The Book on
BOUNDLESS
COURAGE

How to Overcome the Challenges of a Relationship or Get Out of it!

JACINTH SALMON-BRISSETT

Co-authored with
RAYMOND AARON

 AuthoritiesPress

The Book on Boundless Courage: How to Overcome the Challenges of a Relationship or Get Out of it!

www.couragebooknow.com

Copyright © 2020 Jacinth Salmon-Brissett

ISBN: 978-1-77277-366-8

Limits of Liability and Disclaimer of Warranty

The author and publisher shall not be liable for your misuse of the enclosed material. This book is strictly for informational and educational purposes only.

Warning – Disclaimer

The purpose of this book is to educate and entertain. The author and/or publisher do not guarantee that anyone following these techniques, suggestions, tips, ideas, or strategies will become successful. The author and/or publisher shall have neither liability nor responsibility to anyone with respect to any loss or damage caused, or alleged to be caused, directly or indirectly by the information contained in this book.

Medical Disclaimer

Any medical or health information in this book is provided as an information resource only and is not to be used or relied on for diagnostic or treatment purposes. This information is not intended to be patient education, does not create any patient-physician relationship, and should not be used as a substitute for professional diagnosis and treatment.

Publisher
10-10-10 Publishing
Markham, ON
Canada

Printed in Canada and the United States of America

Dedication

The Book on Boundless Courage is specifically dedicated to my daughter, **MizYen**. While observing the insatiable relationship challenges being endured by her mother, she would persistently urge and encourage me to get up and go. MizYen has, herself, demonstrated the courage to listen to the voice within her, to get up and go on those urgings, despite the mountains of difficulties that were visible ahead of her. The progress she now makes is a result of that ability to listen, and to respond positively to that inner voice. This book encourages everyone in a relationship, of whatever nature, to listen to their own still, small, inner voice. Boundless courage lies there.

I dedicate this book also to my very honorable friend and confidante: **May Whittley**. May was the wife of Pastor Victor Whittley of the Mount Salem Open Bible Church in Montego Bay, Jamaica and recently passed. May and I met 13 years ago through travel arranged for us by **Michelle Martin**, mother of my past student of Cornwall College and now Crown Counsel in the Office of the Director of Public Prosecutions, **Malike Kellier**. When May perceived I was passing through the valley of despair, she took me under her wings, massaged my soul with incomparable compassion, bridged me back to sanity and supported me until the day of her death. May has now gifted me her family, and I owe her a debt of gratitude and remembrance.

Additionally, I dedicate this book as a source of inspiration to young people who are starting out on the relationship-building journey, and particularly to women and men in challenged relationships. When you buy this book, read this book, share this book, or talk about this book, you will discover that *The Book on Boundless Courage* is for anyone who wishes to topple the perplexing thought that "the more things change, the more they remain the same." The truth is that nothing has to remain the same; our relationships get better when we listen to the voice of positivity within us, and act upon it for better and not for worse.

It is important to note that our environment is loaded with the clang and the clash and bang and bash of noises all around us. We are indeed bombarded and forced to listen to everything except the gift of our own inner voices. This book urges all of us to muster the courage to listen amidst the indomitable confusion that abounds around us. It is the battle of the survival of the fittest; and our courage—our boundless courage—will break the cords that bind us to defeat, failure, and fear. Just do courage!

Table of Contents

Table of Contents

Acknowledgments

Did you know that gratitude is the rent we pay for the space we occupy on earth? Against this background, I am taking time out to ensure I pay my dues.

Firstly, I acknowledge the **Raymond Aaron** group and the 10-10-10 Writer's Program. You have enabled me to make this dream of writing a book the reality it has become today. Thank you, Raymond, for co-authoring this book with me.

I wish to also acknowledge the dedicated support of **Tracy Knepple**, who worked tirelessly with me, helping me to unearth and vocalize my experiences so that they became easier to solidify into this tangible form.

Thanks too, to all the important people who have touched my life in one way or another: Old Boys of Cornwall College: past students of the school on the hill beside the sea, members of the speech and drama clubs, members of the Spanish club, and members of the Culture club. Those were the best days of my journey as a teacher, advising and coordinating your programs and activities.

I especially want to acknowledge past student, **Joseph Farquharson**, who still remembers my birthday. It warms my heart to be remembered in a special way, and from as far away as Germany. Though our paths have split, **Malike Kellier** still ensures his mother takes good care of my travel and lodging arrangements whenever I travel to the island. Thanks a lot Malike. **Thura Soe Htwe** has taken time out from his family and busy schedule to connect with me on Facebook. That is awesome! **Calbert Graham** has connected with me out of the United Kingdom. It is amazing to be in touch with you.

I acknowledge the kindness of my brothers and sisters: **Roger, Dewey, Joe, Spencer, George, Marcia,** and **Merle**. Special mention also for my immensely helpful nieces: **Annmarie** and **Alethia Clarke**.

I also want to acknowledge some extra special neighbors and colleagues: **Evvy Jenoure, Carlito Somera, Raphael Adeniyi, Edel Paracuelles, Lori Aliche, Charmaine Harrison, Charmaine Chennis, Beverly** and **Sharon Austin, Paulet** and **George Harty** and family, **Blossome McLaughlin-Allen** and family. Thank you for your consistent strong words of encouragement to me.

Acknowledgments

To **Karen Colquhoun-Wallace**, thank you for being my persistent source of incredibly positive encouragement and a believer in my power and ability to produce a masterpiece. Karen, you make me wonder how you see beyond my façade of fear to highlight what seems hidden and out of sight.

A special thank you to **MizYen**, my one and only daughter, who believes her mother can move any mountain that confronts her. Thank you also to **Aion**, my one and only son, whose support with my Airbnb endeavor frees up time for me to dedicate to this important project. Thank you, **Mama Isola Baker**, for ensuring that I learned to read, write, and support myself. You laid the foundation for my life, out of which this book has come.

Thank you to my colleague of many years past, **Pearlina Fray**, now resident in the Bahamas. I was lucky to track her down through an old email address. As we talked of old times over the phone, trying to fill in the gap years, Pearlina felt that my stories merited preservation within the covers of a book. Her urgings were stronger than an encouragement, and that helped me realize the importance of immortalizing my stories. Thank you, Pearlina.

Thanks also to **Glen** and **Ingrid Gregory**, whose care of my property in Ontario has not only allowed me to survive here in Alberta but has also positively impacted my ability to make this book happen. I owe you a debt of gratitude. Thank you so much!

To my incredibly special friend, **Bola**, and her husband, **Dr. Peter Mebude**, who, since I met them in 2009, have not said no to anything I have asked of them. This couple graciously accepted the challenge to critically proofread my script while I worked on editing it. I am extremely grateful for your support. Thank you very, very much.

Thank you to **Ms. Jennifer Gorkoff**, present principal of Jack James High School, who understood the request I made to be temporarily released to participate in a three-day book-writing workshop in Toronto. Thanks also to **Catherine Forbes**, past acting principal of **Jack James** along with **Michelle Konschuh**, and **Warren Ferguson**, who managed the school in 2018 when I arrived there as a substitute teacher. Your recognition of my gifting as an educator, and as a caring, compassionate teacher, led you to recommend me unhesitatingly to be meaning-fully contracted with the Calgary Board of Education, for which I am tremendously grateful.

I also acknowledge **Diane Thorsell** and **Debbie Twomey**, the two EAs who guided, supported, and helped me make a success of a challenging year of baptism in the PLP program. Thanks also to **Kathy Whitehead**, the business office manager, for being patient and understanding with me on my numerous trips to get her help to navigate the accounts for my department. Thanks to **Valerie Tiller** and **Sharon Hube Whitman**, the front desk ladies who supported me from start to finish. You are amazing!

Jack James High School is the closest I have come to experiencing a feeling of family in all the years I have spent in Calgary. My experiences there surpass expectations, with **Pamela Blake** who cleaned the snow from my car; **Tony Liu**, my ever present support with IT; **Matthew Penman**, a ready support for the youth in my program; the staff who included me on lunch-out moments; **Dean Bittman**, who transported my class on all our bussed trips; and **Sarah Hargreaves**, the grad organizer, and **Jamie Willis**, the Aboriginal grad coach, who ensured I was included in school activities. I also want to acknowledge the Culinary department of the school specially, for preparing and serving the best meals I have had so far, anywhere in Calgary. If you are blessed to work at this illustrious school, know that I thank you for having touched my life while our paths crossed. It is my hope that **Jack James** would retain and build upon the essence of good that it embodies.

I would be remiss for not thanking a special group of persons who supported me while I worked at Jack James: **Matt Zinken**, Area 3 Special Needs Strategist; **Crystal Gatza**, PLP teacher at Ernest Morrow Middle School; **Barbara Hare** and **Shawn Powell**, PLP teachers at Forest Lawn High School; **Sandra Cowley**, PLP teacher at

Robert Thirsk High School; and **Nicole Pasquarelli**, PLP teacher at the Bowness High School. Thank you for the support you freely and willingly gave me throughout the year I worked in the PLP program.

Additionally, I want to thank **Heidi Lutz** and **Tammy Quiring** for your sincere support throughout the year I spent at the Lester B. Pearson High School. Please know that I appreciate you for all you did. I want to also mention two other CBE schools: Escuela Collingwood and the Dalhousie Elementary, where I believe I worked most while I taught as a substitute teacher. Know that I sincerely miss the camaraderie we shared while I worked alongside you. Also to the very helpful and supportive staff of the Queen Elizabeth High School, where I worked on a temporary contract, thank you for allowing me to walk forward with the confidence I needed to face the world when that contract ended.

My ability to navigate and weather the storms of life is due in part to the foundation of faith that has been deposited in me. Against that background, I take time out here to thank the following assemblies and leaders: **Bishop Reuben Macpherson** and the Pentecostal Assemblies of Jesus in Jamaica, **Bishop Orville Rodney** and the church at Valencia Drive, the **Reverend Vivian Burke** and the church at 11 Elgin Road, **Bishop Kenroy** and **Lady Pamela Morris** and the church at 251 King William Street, **Pastor Henry Thompson** and the church at Centre Street, **Bishop Gerald Johnson** and **Pastor Joy Johnson-Green** and the Showers of Blessing Church in Calgary. Thank you for rightly dividing the fortifying word of God.

Also, to my newly-made librarian friend, **Irina Horvath**, who graciously agreed to take a critical look at my cover and who, in turn, gave me an honest assessment of it, I want to say a special thank you.

The authority I have become today hinges upon the support I have enjoyed from various other groups, relatives, and friends, among which is the **Substitute Teachers' Group of the Calgary Board of Education**. Thank you for allowing me to work along with you, holding positions and supporting our colleagues as we struggle together to find our place in the education system.

Thanks, also, to **John** and **Oby Igbiki** and the Glory Awakening Fellowship, which has allowed me to expand my network of connections while building up my faith and trust in our father, God.

In addition, I thank my **Aunt Mercie** and **Uncle Jos**, who organized and supported the transition of my children and me to Canada. Thank you wholeheartedly. Thanks, too, to **Auntie Marr** and **Stephen** and **Uncle Harry** and **Courtney**, for making their home in Mississauga the central place for everyone named or connected as a

Salmon to converge once we arrive in Canada. You are amazing and I thank you!

And, to **Ines Rios** and **Elizabeth Webb** and the indomitable team at the, now, Immigrants Working Centre, who invited me to join them in the Orientation to the Labour Market, coached and mentored me to become a Canadian worker, and then hired me and gave me my first full-time job in Canada, I thank you very much. Words are insufficient to adequately thank you for reaching out and touching lives like mine. Thanks a million!

Finally, to all who will purchase, read, share, discuss, give life and movement to this book once it is published, thank you very, very much.

Foreword

Relationships are complicated, and require you to stand up for yourself while providing support and love to others. The biggest challenge often is one of determining when a relationship requires immediate intervention as opposed to when a relationship has become so critically unhealthy that you need to find closure. In *The Book on Boundless Courage: How to Overcome the Challenges of a Relationship or Get Out of it!*, Jacinth Salmon-Brissett shares life lessons garnered from years of dealing with a relationship that was doubtlessly unhealthy.

As she shares her experiences, Jacinth also gives you the necessary tools and skills to assess your own relationship and make informed directional decisions based on the data you uncover. *The Book on Boundless Courage* focuses on not only how to be resolute for your relationship, but also how to be courageous for yourself. Jacinth shares the importance of personal peace, and why it is necessary to be willing to step back from engaging in negatively charged emotional states of conflict.

Jacinth does not just encourage you to assess your relationship's health and wellness; she also dives into the skills necessary to make a relationship work, and how to fix unhealthy habits and routines for the betterment of your bond. Her book serves as a guide for giving your relationship a chance to return to health and prosperity, even after extremely difficult challenges.

The Book on Boundless Courage is not only a guide, but one woman's story to find peace for herself and her children in challenging circumstances. Not only does Jacinth share her journey; she inspires you to make changes in your own life, to improve your own relationship and to find the courage to move on from an unhealthy situation to what you desire and deserve. Along the way, Jacinth also reminds you to continue to show love for yourself and for others, with practical tips on how to discuss problems with your partner, or de-escalate an emotional situation.

While some of her advice mirrors thoughts in other relationship books, Jacinth brings a fresh twist with her focus on love and peace, as well as the importance of creating relationships that support you in finding that love and that peace, which are so desirable for successful relationships. She gives you the tools to prioritize your life, allowing you to shift your focus from the material aspects of a relationship to the deeper emotional, mental, and spiritual ones.

Foreword

If you have reached the place where you are ready to get honest with yourself about the health of your relationship, then *The Book on Boundless Courage: How to Overcome the Challenges of a Relationship or Get Out of it!* is the guide you have been waiting for!

Loral Langemeier
The Millionaire Maker

1

Where is Your Relationship Right Now?

1

Today's world is built upon the relationships we have with ourselves and others. Understanding more about our relationships helps us to evaluate whether a relationship is working or not. Part of the journey of any relationship is coming to a deeper understanding of yourself and others. Throughout this book, I want you to identify the areas of your relationship where you might be struggling, and use the information here to help you improve it.

Any change is going to start with you and how you act or react to different circumstances. Throughout the following chapters, we are going to focus on learning more about who you are and how you impact your relationship in positive or negative ways. If you recently got out of a relationship, I want you to recognize that you can take your experiences from that relationship, and the tools in this book, to positively impact your next relationship.

Let's start by assessing your current relationship or your recent past one.

Relationship Quiz 1

This activity will help you understand how well your relationship is working. Every relationship needs to be cared for to help it get stronger and healthier. This is not a diagnostic test, but what it will do is help you to gain insight on where your relationship sits at present, and where to focus your next steps. Do you need to focus on your intimacy, or on your passion, or on your commitment to the relationship? These are suggestions to positively help your relationship get better.

Answer the following questions honestly and truthfully, based on your personal experience. Your first choice will be the most authentic, so do not go back and change your answers.

Where is Your Relationship Right Now?

Answer yes/no to reveal the strength of your relationship:

1. We fight.   ❑ Yes ❑ No

2. We argue.   ❑ Yes ❑ No

3. We threaten to quit.   ❑ Yes ❑ No

4. We tell the world about our
    struggles.   ❑ Yes ❑ No

5. I pack up my partner's things and
    put them out.   ❑ Yes ❑ No

6. I pack up and return home to my
    mother.   ❑ Yes ❑ No

7. I get counselling and act upon it.   ❑ Yes ❑ No

8. I demand that my partner gets
    counselling.   ❑ Yes ❑ No

9. I want my family together forever.   ❑ Yes ❑ No

10. I am concerned about the children.   ❑ Yes ❑ No

11. I worry about money.   ❑ Yes ❑ No

12. I feel uncared for.   ❑ Yes ❑ No

13. I feel despised.   ❑ Yes ❑ No

14. I feel disrespected.   ❑ Yes ❑ No

15. I express my feelings.   ❏ Yes   ❏ No

16. I feel I made a very grave choice
    for this relationship.   ❏ Yes   ❏ No

17. I break things.   ❏ Yes   ❏ No

18. I am angry inside.   ❏ Yes   ❏ No

19. We don't go out together.   ❏ Yes   ❏ No

20. I feel rejected.   ❏ Yes   ❏ No

21. I ask for a divorce.   ❏ Yes   ❏ No

22. I think of bad things to do to my
    partner.   ❏ Yes   ❏ No

23. I pray and fast.   ❏ Yes   ❏ No

24. I starve myself.   ❏ Yes   ❏ No

25. I have no hope.   ❏ Yes   ❏ No

16 – 25 yeses: Speak with a lawyer

10 – 15 yeses: See a marriage counsellor

5 – 9 yeses: Go on a couples' retreat

0 – 8 yeses: Keep on doing what you're doing

Relationship Quiz 2

In this quiz, I want you to focus on your reactions to your partner. Respond with a yes/no, and remember to just put your first answer.

1. I think about my spouse night and day. ❑ Yes ❑ No

2. I will let no one come between us. ❑ Yes ❑ No

3. I do not judge my partner based on assumptions or what I hear. ❑ Yes ❑ No

4. I share my deep personal information about myself. ❑ Yes ❑ No

5. We have a romantic, sexual relationship. ❑ Yes ❑ No

6. I correct my partner lovingly and respectfully. ❑ Yes ❑ No

7. I know my love will last forever. ❑ Yes ❑ No

8. I communicate respectfully with my partner. ❑ Yes ❑ No

9. I trust my spouse and have faith in him/her. ❑ Yes ❑ No

10. I cannot imagine being a partner to another person. ❑ Yes ❑ No

11. I can fully trust my partner. ❑ Yes ❑ No

12. I foster a passionate, giving relationship. ❑ Yes ❑ No

13. I love my partner for life. ❑ Yes ❑ No

14. My spouse understands me. ❑ Yes ❑ No

15. I am completely responsible for my partner. ❑ Yes ❑ No

16. I prefer being with my partner 24/7. ❑ Yes ❑ No

17. My relationship is strong but stale. ❑ Yes ❑ No

18. We talk, talk, talk. ❑ Yes ❑ No

19. We have a life full of sex. ❑ Yes ❑ No

20. We frequently resolve our own issues. ❑ Yes ❑ No

Now I want you to keep in mind the list of areas in your relationship where you have several "no" answers. Those are the areas that you need to focus on as we go through the following chapters. One thing to also keep in mind is that each part of this book is meant to build toward the next chapter and the next set of skills.

Take the time to read this book completely through, and then go back and pick specific chapters to focus on. In addition, I have provided spaces for your notes, at the end of each chapter. Feel free to use this as a relationship workbook. As you read, think about how each of the points could be applied to your relationship. You might find that you have already mastered some areas, but recognize that you are going to identify weaknesses along the way.

I am also going to share how to identify when a relationship needs to end. Not everything is a deal-breaker, yet it is important to understand when your relationship may have entered an unhealthy phase. By understanding where you are in your relationship, and being able to learn from it, you can grow and shine. Let's get started!

NOTES

_____

_____

_____

_____

_____

_____

_____

_____

_____

_____

_____

_____

_____

_____

2

The Challenges of a Relationship

2

If I were to ask you to list your 5 best relationships, I am sure that it would only take you a few minutes to do so. You could probably give me a never-ending list of what makes those relationships so special and important to you. Clearly, there is a strong foundation that underlies these relationships, which is set to help you overcome the various challenges that you might have faced over the course of time.

On the flip side, when a relationship is struggling, listing your challenges can be much easier to do. Right now, I want to concentrate on those challenges, because throughout the rest of this book, we are going to focus on some tools you may need to effectively manage challenges. As you read, note the challenges that speak to you, either because you have experienced them in the past or because you are dealing with them right now.

Along with giving you tools to address the challenges, I am also going to ask you to look at your relationships from a different perspective. It is about seeing the good, as well as the bad of each of your specific challenges. Keep in mind that these challenges are not limited to your romantic relationships but can also be a part of relationships in other areas of your personal and professional life. Let's get started!

Lack of Communication

The challenge to communicate impacts virtually every relationship that you have. When you experience a lack of communication, it makes both parties in the relationship feel isolated and alone. Here are a few of the ways a lack of communication manifests itself. You might find that you both tend to argue back and forth without resolving any issues. In fact, small things tend to trigger big arguments. Even if you don't have big fights, there is the constant bickering that comes from not successfully resolving a problem but rather attacking each other instead.

Lack of communication leads to focusing only on what is going wrong, instead of what is going right. Time and again, misunderstandings grow because each side is interested in defending their position, to the detriment of providing a remedy for the problem.

The frequency of incorrect communication, or lack of communication, emerges from a focus on making your own personal point and not being open to hearing the concerns and needs of the other person. This approach saps the binding love and connection from a relationship, and leaves both of you wondering why you stay together at all.

Infidelity

For relationships that deal with infidelity, there may be other underlying issues that lead to this phenomenon. It could be an emotional relationship. If you build a deeper connection with someone other than your spouse or partner, this is called emotional infidelity. While emotional infidelity does not necessarily have a physical incident attached to it, there is a level of intimacy involved that can trigger a sense of betrayal to your partner or spouse.

Physical infidelity is equally as devastating as emotional infidelity. When a spouse or partner deals with the emotional fallout from the sexual act and the physical connections that were made outside of the relationship, this leads to a lack of trust and a loss of intimacy. There are also other consequences, such as contracting an STD and gifting it to your partner, or the creation of an outside child. All these consequences are more than a relationship can bear, and are primary reasons for ending a relationship.

If you are dealing with these challenges in your current relationship, you may be wondering whether to repair the relationship or to end it. Later, I will talk about how to know when it is time to end a relationship, including some points to keep in mind as you make your decision.

Disrespect and Dishonor

Disrespect in a relationship involves speaking negatively with others about your spouse or partner, or even doing so in front of your partner and your children. It demonstrates that you have little respect for your spouse or partner, and others sense that they can talk negatively to and about your partner as well. The result is that your partner feels degraded, and your children imbibe and internalize this negative trend of thought. They now think it is okay for them to treat their own parent in this way, and later in life, their own partners as well.

If you are showing disrespect to your partner, then you are likely doing so in other relationships, including those with your children. You are impacting the vulnerable mindset of your young children. Continual disrespect compounds feelings of low self-worth. This leads to poor decisions regarding the type of treatment children grow up willing to accept.

Dishonor goes hand in hand with disrespect, as it focuses on degrading your partner by using derogatory terms to describe them, or refusing to use their name when referring to them. You might also choose to call them unkind names, while trying to hurt them and make them feel that they are worthless. While these behaviors might reflect a hurt, or your own feelings of low self-worth, the fact is that by not healing your own issues, you are negatively impacting everyone around you, especially your partner and your own children.

Verbal/Mental/Emotional/Financial Abuse

These types of abuse tend to focus on making your partner feel less valuable and less worthy of your love and affection. They wonder what is wrong with them, because you claim to love them, yet you talk to them in such demeaning ways, and also withhold your affection for arbitrary reasons. Abuse in any form takes a toll on your partner and makes them doubt themselves. All types of abuse contribute to feelings of low self-worth and negative self-talk. When combined, these types lead to psychological abuse, and your partner begins to think of themselves as going crazy.

I want to be clear that these types are not the same as physical abuse. They do not leave the kind of evidence that physical abuse does; but mental, verbal, emotional, and financial abuse often have a more devastating impact on the individual over a longer period. The consequences are more damaging because they leave individuals struggling with feelings of low self-worth for years or for life. Even if you end the abuse by ending the relationship, you often find yourself bringing the impact of the abuse into your other relationships. Those who deal with these types of abuse need additional assistance to heal themselves afterwards. They also need a solid support system and counseling so that they can begin to heal their mind and their spirit.

Lack of Sex/Intimacy

This matter is challenging because when a partner does not get their needs for intimacy met in the relationship, they often seek other ways to meet these basic needs. The result is infidelity or the ending of one relationship to move to another, where the need for intimacy is seemingly met. Hurt feelings and destruction of trust are just two of the results from a lack of intimacy and lack of sex in the relationship.

On the other hand, you might be having physical sex, but not connecting with each other intimately. The physical needs may be met, but the romance and connection that it should bring are missing. The intimacy of the relationship is being withheld. You might have a partner who frequently opts to come to bed in their day clothes and shoes, or may just go right to sleep without acknowledging you or without spending a few minutes caring for your needs.

Partners who deal with a lack of romance, and a lack of intimacy, find themselves feeling neglected and taken advantage of, to the point that they become burnt out and harbor feelings of being underappreciated. The neglect of intimacy and romance easily and quickly snowballs into a contribution of distrust by both parties. The effect is devastating. The growth is enormous and undesirable. Beware!

When you withhold intimacy, your partner questions why they are in the relationship, and they wonder what is wrong with them. The lack of sex and intimacy negatively impacts both partners, leaving them feeling alone and frustrated. The reality is that ignoring this challenge leads to other challenges, which are even harder to overcome.

Blaming/Accusing/Assuming

These areas are full of negative expressions such as I can't, I won't, or I don't. When you are blaming or accusing, the focus is on what someone else does wrong. You are not acknowledging how your choices and actions have contributed to the situation. Relationships are a two-way street, and there is no such thing as an innocent partner or a guilty one. Both partners play a role in the health and well-being of the relationship, whether they choose to acknowledge their role or not.

Assuming is another way to bring negativity into your relationship. You might be assuming that your partner thinks and feels a certain way and is acting accordingly. Here are the problems with that. One, you don't know for sure what your partner thinks or feels. Two, by acting on your assumptions, you are hurting your partner and causing the misunderstanding to grow bigger. You are also irreparably damaging your worthy relationship.

In the end, blaming, accusing, and assuming will negatively impact your relationship, and divide you and your partner. This division will expand and grow if it is not dealt with right away. Division can turn into a chasm so wide that your wonderful relationship ends with both of you feeling angry, misunderstood, and frustrated. That emotional and mental anguish could be avoided, but by opting to focus on being right, instead of attempting to understand your partner, the pain is established, and the relationship suffers.

Dishonesty

There are so many ways to be dishonest in a relationship. Dishonesty can include being untrue about how you are spending your time, to how you are spending your money. The point is that dishonesty breeds distrust. Once you start feeding your relationship with dishonesty, you are destroying the foundation, the very core and fabric of the relationship, one lie at a time.

There are several areas where dishonesty comes into play in a relationship. For instance, if you own a business together or have mutual investments, and your partner opts to make decisions without consulting you, or chooses to hide some funds from these investments, this builds a pitfall for the bond. Once the deception is discovered, you will begin to question whether your partner is still committed to the relationship or if they are preparing to depart.

Relationships that appear to survive for a while in this scenario, will implode as one partner's dishonesty is discovered by the other. With one partner constantly questioning the other, always on the lookout for discrepancies, an explosion is imminent. One partner has become the parent or police, and the other is either a child or a criminal. No one wants to live like that. By not addressing dishonesty, unearthing the reasons behind it, or exposing the feeling of being trapped or controlled, your relationship is doomed to failure and frustration.

The Lack of Privacy/Sincerity/Trust

Part of the reality of the lack of privacy, sincerity, and trust is that they illustrate the missing connection between two individuals in a relationship. If you lack sincerity in your relationship, then making time for the relationship becomes secondary to pursuing your desires or needs. Doing so, often means that there is a lack of community and support for each other.

After all, if you are not making time for each other, then you can't provide support during difficult times. It can be hard to face things as a team if you don't feel like part of a community or team in your relationship. Without that connection, your relationship becomes two separate people going through the motions.

The lack of support also means that making tough choices is done apart, instead of together. Times of grief and loss are those instances where you need the support and community of your partner. When that support and community is not available, it makes an enormously difficult situation that's much harder to deal with, and even more emotionally draining than any other life experience.

Another issue that many couples contend with is having multiple people fixing their relationship for them. In-laws and friends can become privy to details that are only meant for the individuals in the relationship. As a result, boundaries are crossed, and disrespect rears its ugly head. Expect those same in-laws or friends to also try to put their two cents in, regarding what direction the relationship needs to take.

Clearly, boundaries need to be respected. When boundaries are not regarded, your relationship flounders. It becomes an even greater betrayal of privacy when your partner is actively sharing details of your life and plans with random individuals, or with someone with whom they are forming a romantic attachment or building an emotional affair.

Lack of privacy is a betrayal of trust. If a partner shares some things that are close to their heart, and you in turn choose to share those intimate details with others, there is a sense of betrayal. Over time, that sense of betrayal mounts, and partners find themselves unwilling to share in and contribute to the intimacy in the relationship. They can't but wonder who else is learning about the intimate aspects of the relationship. The relationship is now clouded with fear and doubt, and your sincerity and loyalty are called to question.

You can now easily see how most of these challenges contribute to a lack of trust. If you feel that you can't trust your partner, you are going to try to protect yourself, and that underwrites the growing divide between the two of you.

Malice

Do you find that your partner tends to disappear for days on end without letting you know? Where are they? Perhaps they are using silence to punish you for both real and imagined infractions. Refusing to talk to each other adds to the struggle to address issues. You can't have a conversation with someone who refuses to talk and makes themselves absent even when they are sitting in front of you.

Disappearing is also malicious. It is mentally exhausting. If you care, you easily worry that your partner might be hurt or lost. For partners who disappear and leave no money for food or bills, one wonders what they are thinking. You are left to figure out, all on your own, how to survive without resources, and with the gifting of sleepless nights and worrisome days, not knowing when or if your partner will return. It is a frightful state to be in.

The irony is that throughout each of these challenges, one partner or both is/are trying to defend themselves at the cost of the relationship. One or both are not open to learning something, or are neglecting to address the issues. Both would rather be right. You are blocking communication, and you can't hear what your partner is concerned about. They may have a valid point, but you are too busy defending your own position to stop and listen.

Clearly, addressing any of these challenges is going to require an open mind and heart. You must be willing to hear and make changes to be successful. With that in mind, I want to help you shift your mental viewpoint. Throughout this chapter, we have shown how these challenges can negatively impact your relationship, and be damaging to your emotional and physical well-being.

We are all responsible for caring for our own mental and physical well-being. When a relationship is challenged, your own well-being is negatively impacted. That is the reason I want to focus on the good that some challenges can bring to your relationship. Many challenges serve as our wake-up call, and this is a definite positive, so race with me to the next chapter, where we will look more closely at the positive impact that challenges can have on a relationship.

NOTES

_____

_____

_____

_____

_____

_____

_____

_____

_____

_____

_____

_____

_____

_____

3

The Good in Relationship Challenges

3

In Chapter 2, I talked about several relationship challenges and how these challenges negatively impact our ability to connect with our partners. However, you might be shocked to learn that some of those same challenges can also help you to grow, both as an individual and also within your relationship. I call them the "good" of challenges.

To see the good in any challenge, you must first shift your perception of that challenge. While the difficulties in your relationship cause you grave concern, those challenges also point out the weak areas in your relationship that need immediate attention. Too often, we focus on how challenges negatively impact us, while we neglect to pay attention to what they are teaching us about ourselves, our partners, and our relationships. Nevertheless, these challenges are our wake-up call. They allow us to better understand ourselves, our needs, and the needs of our partner.

Learning From a Lack of Communication

One of the things I want to highlight here is that when both partners are talking, and there is very little listening taking place, all that talk does nothing to improve the state of your relationship. Neither are you or your partner being heard. A still tongue keeps a wise head; knowing when to be quiet and when to speak up are skills that can help you understand what is going on behind the harsh words being spoken to or by your partner.

You must be willing to bite your tongue (not literally, of course), especially when you feel that strong urge to respond right away to the things your partner is saying. To activate your listening capacity, allow your partner to get everything out without you interrupting, and do your best to not take anything personally. For instance, if your partner is impatient with you in the evenings, it is very probable that the issue has nothing to do with you or with your home, but has everything to do with the stresses and frustrations related to their work environment. They may already have been irritated before coming home, and now any small thing easily becomes a trigger to their negative responses. Now, they blurt out unkind things, and you need to be wise and kind to not blurt back, because a soft answer turns away anger, and a still tongue keeps a wise head.

At this moment of concern, it is wise to shift your viewpoint to recognize that perhaps your partner's frustration has nothing to do with you. After they have vented and calmed down, try to ask some questions to clarify the situation and to show that you were truly listening to what they had to say. After the initial vent, they may find themselves in a better position to discuss their concerns and to share the true source of their frustration with you.

So, practice being quiet while allowing your partner to express themselves, and then bring the matter up later, in a quieter time period. Many times, the situation escalates because neither partner has assumed the role of listener. Perhaps the lack of communication in your relationship is signaling to you that it is time to listen more, and with an open heart and mind. If your partner is lacking in this area, try to focus instead on improving your own listening skills. Your positive choice and action will produce a positive shift in your partner as well. Isn't this what you want?

Another good thing that relationship challenges produce is a sensitivity to your own communication style versus your partner's. Each partner has a unique way of expressing themselves. When you don't feel heard, it often is because your communication style is clashing with your partner's.

Here is a simple example. If you are a direct individual who sees a problem or issue and want to deal with it right then and there, you will not want to wait until later for a discussion. You want to talk with your partner right away. You also want them to immediately share their feelings and their insights and their possible solutions.

Your partner, on the other hand, wants to step away from the situation or issue, to give themselves time to process their emotional response. They require time to meditate on what they want to say. Neither response is wrong, but you can see how frustration occurs under these circumstances.

The partner who wants to address the matter right away may feel that their partner is dismissing the importance of the issue by saying things like, "Let's talk about this later." They may feel hurt. They could feel as if their partner is not making the relationship a priority. On the other hand, the partner who wants time to process the situation before talking about it may also feel bullied by the other, and may lash out angrily if they feel pushed or rushed.

My children are dealing with various trauma related to the breakup of our family. Sometimes my daughter goes off the handle, regurgitating negative feelings and frustrations. At other times, she just lets everything out. During those spills, I have opted to not say anything, to not criticize, to not interject, to not comment. I simply let her get it off her chest. I allow her to vent until she has got out everything that she needs to say.

Later, she comes back and apologizes for the fiery outbursts. This is the opportunity I capitalize on to talk about our situation as calmly and as quietly as possible, and then we move forward with a better feeling about each other. I strongly believe a still tongue keeps a wise head. This approach makes my daughter feel she is being listened to and that she has a safe place to share what is bothering her. Now, that doesn't give license to anyone to angrily attack others. What that does is to allow others the free rein to express their emotions and thoughts without censor. This is a great way to learn more about your partner. In the end, you can better address the real underlying issues, with both of you feeling heard and valued.

In both instances, a lack of communication has revealed an area where you and your partner need to make changes. While you are not in charge of your partner, you can use this information to help you grow, regardless of the choices that your partner makes. This point will come into play throughout this book, and will help you make yourself accountable for your actions and your choices.

Can There Be Good in Infidelity?

You might be ready to jump up right now and shout, "What good can there be in a cheating partner?" I agree that there is plenty of sadness, hurt, anger, and grieving that occurs when one partner chooses to step outside of the relationship, to engage in an emotional or a physical affair. There can be hours of wondering what you lacked that made your partner stray, or you may be questioning their love for you. When trust is shattered, there is always a struggle to rebuild it. You may even find that it is impossible to rebuild it again.

However, within all these negative consequences, you can start to find out some important things about yourself and your partner. For instance, if your partner frequently chooses to have emotional affairs outside your union, what might be lacking in the relationship so that their needs are not being met? Perhaps you realize that both of you are feeling isolated and unhappy because one or more of your needs are not being met in the relationship.

This may be the wake-up call you both need to expect better from your partner, but also to reach out and make your needs clearly known. After all, your partner is not a mind reader. Tell them what you want from the relationship. Share your needs and your goals. Visualize your future, and share your thoughts with your partner.

Infidelity can serve to be a wake-up call regarding the state of your relationship, as well as areas that you both need to improve on. A relationship, which has broken down to the point that one person is looking outside for understanding and companionship, needs healing and a recognition of what you are doing or are not doing to make the relationship better.

As a wounded partner, it is hard to hear that your partner opted to look outside your relationship to fill their emotional or physical needs. While they are responsible for their choices, it is important to still examine your own self. Did you ignore the blatant issues or push your partner away? Were you hurting and isolating yourself? Did you leave your partner to feel unwanted?

Perhaps you assumed that your partner wouldn't understand your needs, so you simply opted to get them filled elsewhere. Assuming the worst of your partner, or thinking negatively of them on a regular basis, can impact your desire to stay true to your partner. You are still in charge of your choices. When you turn away from your relationship, you are still accountable for the consequences that result. However, if both of you are willing to work on the relationship, then the healing from infidelity can involve rebuilding your relationship to make it stronger and better.

Here are a few of the ways that your relationship can improve:

Better communication – Talking about your concerns and needs instead of ignoring them or looking outside the relationship.

Learn to address the molehills before they become mountains – Too often, little issues can get ignored in a relationship, but they become the seeds of larger problems. Address them right away, and your relationship will benefit.

Change how you deal with each other – It can be hard to change the dynamics of your relationship, but once you address the root causes behind the breakdown, you can shift the dynamics of your relationship for the better.

Learn to support each other – Part of the healing process includes becoming a soft place to fall for your partner. As you rebuild trust, then you are also rebuilding the support system that is a critical part of your relationship.

Clearly, dealing with infidelity may involve taking advantage of counseling services and other therapies to help you address issues within your relationship. Doing the work will allow you to be at peace with the decision to stay in the relationship and strengthen it, or to end it and walk away.

The Good of Relationship Challenges

No matter what the challenge (and I listed several in Chapter 2), the point is that each of these challenges can give you an opportunity to learn more about yourself and your partner. Challenges help you to identify the weaknesses and strengths in your relationship. When you can identify the challenges, you can also make the conscious choice to own them and fix them, individually and as a team.

By recognizing your challenges, you give yourself a path of action to make your relationship better. When your relationship appears to be going smoothly, then you have less of a reason to stop and look at it. Maintenance on a relationship is necessary but can be easy to neglect when there do not appear to be any challenges. However, when you have challenges, those areas that are worn or need attention come to light, and that's good!

Facing challenges allows you to analyze the relationship and see what value it has to you in the present. You are being tested. The relationship is also being tested to see how sturdy it is, what it is standing on, and how it may be fortified. In terms of infidelity, it gives both partners a chance to critically look at the relationship, particularly the things of value. Is it worth keeping? Is it worth fighting for? Should I or should I not let it go?

If your partner is verbally or emotionally abusive, those actions could reflect what they learned in the past and what was modelled for them. As you analyze the relationship, the chance to ask your partner to make changes becomes available to you. This may involve counseling or may force you to make a conscious effort to change how you respond and how you address your partner. If your changes ignite the effort to change in your partner, then that shows they value the relationship. However, if your partner insists on making no adjustments, after you have expressed your concerns and persist on making personal changes, then you are learning more about how much they value the relationship. It is now a personal choice to keep trying or to quit.

If the mirror is held up in front of your face, and you do not like what you see, then you have an opportunity to correct it. When it comes to a relationship, you can make changes to your actions and how you deal with your partner, but in the end, those changes are only going to impact the relationship so far. Your partner needs to be willing to do the work as well. If they aren't, this may be the information you need in order to decide if the relationship is worth additional efforts and counseling to save it.

I want to be clear that no one should have to live with verbal, physical, emotional, or any other type of abuse. It is incumbent upon the man to love his wife as he loves himself, and for the woman, in turn, to respect her partner as the head and leader of her family. If neither partner is willing to effectively assume their role, and is not willing to change negative behaviors, then wisdom says you need to love yourself enough to make the change that removes you from that negative environment. Recognize that not everyone is willing to try; yet when you and your partner both try for better, it is possible to strengthen your relationship and positively address issues or challenges impacting the union.

Remember, you are responsible for yourself and your mental well-being. You as an individual are responsible for taking care of yourself and making sure that you are safe. When you share how you are feeling, then your partner is becoming aware of what you need, and they can then take better care regarding their treatment of you. Everyone is responsible for speaking up and for letting their partner know what works and what does not. If you do so, then you are giving your partner the opportunity to adjust their own approach so that the relationship will work.

These discussions need to happen when both of you are calm. Part of the process involves attacking the issues or challenges without attacking each other. When you get defensive, then your walls go up, and the discussion is not able to benefit either of you. Your ability to hear what others are saying can be restricted when you are in a defensive mode.

To avoid getting defensive, do not assume that your partner is being critical or malicious. Instead, open your mind and heart to what they are saying. After all, it is an emotional discussion for them as well. The point is to hear what the other one is saying with an open mind and heart. That might not be easy, but it is worth doing for the benefit of your relationship. The reality is that both of you may not be in the same place regarding your relationship. One of you could feel it is worth saving, while the other does not, but it is very valid to listen with an open mind. Open discussions allow you to find out where each of you are at, and what you want out of the relationship right now and into the future.

Is it a Block to Communication?

One of the realities of any relationship is that one partner may not be open to communication and could be actively blocking it. You try to open the discussion, but they ignore you or choose to respond negatively. It may be an opportunity to employ quietness. When you do, it gives you the chance to absorb what your partner has said, instead of immediately responding.

Those initial responses can often do more harm than good, by fanning the flames of anger, hurt, and frustration. By employing quietness, you may find the other party coming around and saying, "I see where you are coming from now." If you keep talking, however, you could be blocking the door to anyone hearing what you have to say. Make your point and then let it alone. Give them time to meditate on it, so they can come to you later when they are able to discuss it further in a more favorable way.

Listening and silence are keys to communication. When you let your partner talk it out, giving voice to all their fears and frustrations, you give them the space to express themselves without judgement. Be open to the silence and what it can allow you to learn about your partner when you just let them talk without trying to interject a point or shift the direction of the discussion.

You will find it helpful to interject questions regarding how they feel, but without judgement. Your support for your partner is expressed by listening, by absorbing what they are saying, and allowing them to bring their issues and hurts out into the open. It is surprising how often all your partner needs from you is to have someone listen to them, without offering solutions or a plan of action. It is so valuable to give someone the gift of listening to them while keeping a mental record. If the matter comes back on the table, then that is the time to discuss it further. The heat of the moment may mean it is better to just listen and not respond.

One of the realities of a broken relationship is that people tend to listen to respond, instead of listening to hear and connect with the other individual. In your relationship, listening to hear is a skill that will benefit you and your connection with your partner. When you listen to learn about your partner, you can learn a lot about yourself as well. Too often, we throw up walls and blocks, and focus on what the other person has done, and we assume what their motives are. Being open means not making excuses for yourself but acknowledging how your actions can impact the situation.

Clearly, the good of challenges is that you can look at your relationship with fresh eyes, you can identify potential problems, and you can perceive the blocks in your communication style with your partner. It is a way for you to make changes, and to grow as an individual and as a unit.

Another benefit is that you get to clarify misunderstandings, and grow in unity with each other. You also learn how to be honest with each other, even if it means sharing things that could be painful. The point is to address them for healing and growth to take place. Challenges allow you to acknowledge the good in your partner and affirm your relationship. In the end, positive communication, one of the offshoots of communication challenges, becomes key to healing, and to assist in decision making. Communication helps you critically understand where you are right now, and teaches you to be open to listen, and to listen in silence.

When you are open to communicating and to learn and grow with your partner, you are putting aside faulty pride to build an amazing connection. In line with discussing the good found in relationship challenges, it is critical to understand how you communicate and the potential obstacles that you could be creating in your relationship. As you meditate on your communication style, it is important to look for areas to make changes that will positively impact your relationship. Doing so means that your relationship will grow in ways that will benefit both of you, exponentially and eternally.

NOTES

_____

_____

_____

_____

_____

_____

_____

_____

_____

_____

_____

_____

_____

4

How Do You Communicate With Each Other?

4

No matter what type of relationship you may have with one another, it cannot grow and progress without communication. Both of you are constantly sharing thoughts and feelings, through verbal and non-verbal communication. Your ability to understand how you and your partner communicate is going to be key in building a successful relationship. Why?

Too often, the confusion between partners results from how you communicate with each other. Miscommunication, on the other hand, is the misunderstanding of the communication style of your partner. When you misinterpret what your partner is trying to say, or if you attribute inaccurate meaning to their conversations, you are increasing the likelihood of creating a divide in your relationship.

Throughout the next few pages, I want to talk about how your communication style could clash with that of your partner. Along the way, I want you to bear in mind that assumptions of your partner's motives or intentions often lead to greater challenges than if you were to listen without judgement. Now let's talk about the various styles of communication that exist.

Understanding Your Communication Style

There is a variety of communication styles out there. Each style has its strengths and weaknesses. For instance, one individual may prefer to step away from a hot, emotional discussion that is getting out of control, in order to collect their thoughts and be able to discuss the matter more calmly at a later date or time.

Others may need to complete the discussion right then and there, regardless of how heated the conversation gets. They feel that if the matter is left for a later time, their feelings will fester and, possibly, explode. I want you to stop for a moment and record what you prefer to do when dealing with a stressful conversation. How do you prefer to manage difficult topics? Write your ideas down on the pages at the end of this chapter.

After you have pinned down your own communication style, it is then important to take the time to understand your partner's communication style. After all, you were both raised under two different circumstances and environments, and have experienced two different life-styles. Both of your worlds of experiences, before you started to build a life together, were effectively unique and different. Now you are attempting to merge two different styles of self-expression on yourselves, and that in itself is indeed a challenge.

It is, therefore, important that you both identify your own individual mode of communication and the potential areas where miscommunication may result. A person whose communication style allows them to walk away during conflict could be perceived as ignoring their partner's need to discuss the issue right away. However, the way we communicate is not the problem. The real problem is how we misinterpret the communication style of our partner. The problem is the motives and intentions that we assign to our partners as a result of our misinterpretations. The real issue is knowing how to effect the art of compromise so that an agreement can be reached.

None of us is perfect. None of us knows the magic to instantly and constantly understand another person. However, once you analyse the emotional component, it becomes easier to see and understand how assumptions and snap judgments of what a partner is trying to communicate, may surface.

It's All in the Delivery

Another matter that can lead to misinterpretation of communication is the reading or misreading of the non-verbal body language of your partner. Talk about an easy way to get a mixed message. Your partner, for example, may not look you in the eye during a heated argument. You, on the other hand, may interpret this action to mean a display of insecurity or insincerity, or not paying attention. That judgment is not necessarily true, but your misinterpretation can lead to frustration and a tongue-lashing. A heated counter-response ensues, and then the whole conversation spirals out of control. Wow!! Of course, this is not what you want—you are desirous of harmony in the relationship.

So then, take a moment to think about how you personally tend to carry yourself in conversations with others. How do you hold your head? Do you make eye contact? Do you twitch and turn? Knowing these things about yourself can help you to begin to process how those things might be interpreted by others with whom you communicate. I am not suggesting that you change everything about how you communicate, but rather that you build an awareness of how others may respond or assume your utterances. An awareness of yourself allows you to adjust your responses and prevent more situations from going out of control.

Tone is also an element that often creates friction in relationships. Recognize that you are more likely to get your point across to your partner if you use a sensitive tone. Your message can sound completely different under different tones.

Most women tend to like a soft and gentle tone. Many men also prefer a gentle, smiling partner. A smile is not necessarily physical. A smile can be heard in the tone of your voice. A soft answer, it is said, turns away wrath. This phrase is especially useful when dealing with angry individuals. If you choose a gentle tone during an argument, it diffuses the anger. Once the situation is calmer, it becomes easier to discuss the issue and resolve it. A soft answer is like the lightning strike that diffuses the electrical charge in the air.

Showing that you care by the things you do for your partner is another powerful way to deliver good communication. This type of delivery is often a source of joy for your partner. You are, without words, demonstrating how important your partner is to you. It is much more powerful than getting up every day and saying, "I love you, I love you, I love you." Empty barrels, they say, only make noise. Here are a few actions that communicate your love without using words:

- Helping with chores around the home

- Cooking dinner

- Stepping in to handle the children's schedule

- Allowing your partner to have an evening without chores

It sounds so simple, but all partners appreciate these wordless actions that help them relieve stress and feel cared for. When these seemingly simple things are neglected, it is easy for a partner to see the other as insensitive. The individual feels unloved, unsupported, and neglected. It is, therefore, important to take some time to focus on and analyse how you are delivering your communication. You could find that your message is being misinterpreted in the delivery, or that you are missing out on how you are hurting and neglecting the needs of your partner.

Ask your partner what they think or feel when you respond in a certain way. Allow them to be honest with you. It might be surprising how much you learn about your own style of communication, and also how much you can help your partner to understand about you!

Like misinterpretation and tone, cultural differences can also account for relationship challenges. I am from the Caribbean, where our direct way of communication is different from what I have encountered here in North America. I often feel that I need a cultural interpreter from time to time. To compound this cultural divide, are the differences in communication styles that relate to different religious backgrounds. What is astounding is the frequency with which cross-cultural and cross-religious relationships are being built. In every way, we need to be open-minded and not so quick to judge or take offense. The reality is that when one gets offended, the offence can often be understood through lenses that are cultural or religious. In the final analysis, it is usually found that no true offense was meant, and that through compromise, an apology, and the exercise of true under-standing, the relationship is soon on track again.

Are You a Yeller?

Do you know someone who is always yelling? They yell at their partners. They yell at the children. They yell at their pets. They even yell at the inanimate objects around them. No matter what the situation, they always seem to be yelling. Now, let me ask you, does anyone even listen when someone else is yelling?

The point I want to make here is that yelling is counterproductive. It might get someone's attention, but it is unlikely that they are going to retain much of anything that is said. Instead, you are probably starting to yell back or simply block out the yeller altogether.

When both parties are just yelling and blocking each other out, neither of them is hearing what the other has to say. Do you think the yelling party is going to make the relationship improve and progress? Can the parties address or resolve their questions if they are constantly yelling? Is the relationship likely to get better?

Remember, the soft answer is what dissipates anger and disunity. If your partner is a yeller, or if you are a yeller, then consider using a soft answer instead of yelling back. It might take a few minutes for your partner to realize that you are not yelling, but once they do, that recognition will bring them down from yelling. You can now, essentially, re-open the dialogue again, just by choosing to stop and answer softly. You may also go the route of being silent, but it must be clear that you are very actively listening by looking at the speaker with kindness, and also by not walking away in the heat of the moment.

Now that we have talked about the importance of diffusing the yelling bomb, let's talk about how your communication style can become a defense mechanism.

Communication as a Defense

I know that defense is a critical part of how we function as humans. We want to defend our families, our choices, our actions, and our ideas. If we perceive someone is being critical, we want to defend our stance. While the right delivery can help us accept criticism more tolerably, the truth is that putting up your defenses can happen so quickly that you do not even realize that you have put them up. Yet once those defenses are raised, your hearing is blocked, and communication is hindered.

Part of what I want you to take away from the focus on communication is that you need to be open-minded and not too quick to throw up your defenses. Instead, listen more to understand your partner more. Sometimes we listen to be understood by our partner, and that means the focus is all on us. It is, however, time for you to look outward, focus on what your partner is trying to say, and not necessarily how they are saying it. Try to shift the focus from what or how they are communicating, to what they need you to hear.

Throughout this chapter, I have brought up various scenarios that are focused on different communication styles and the potential barriers partners sometimes come across. Love— true, real, practical love—is the principal thing. So, give love, and be open to tapping into the tools provided through counseling and therapy. Being willing to make changes to how you communicate, demonstrates a love for your partner, and a willingness to work for the benefit of the relationship. If you find yourself constantly on the defensive when talking with your partner, then you might want to consider digging deeper into why you react that way.

If you are feeling misunderstood, it becomes easy to bring negativity into the relationship. I challenge you to stay positive. Even if you feel that the connection between you and your partner is struggling, stay positive.

The reason I want you to stay positive is because negativity breeds more negativity and resentment. It could be the death knell of your relationship if you allow negativity to have a place in your communication with each other. On the other hand, positivity breeds positivity! The impact of positivity on your relationship means that you both feel built up, affirmed, and refreshed after talking with each other.

Take Some and Give Some

Conversation is a two-way street. When you are driving down the road, you can't drive properly if someone is hogging their lane and moving into yours. Conversations are the same way. You cannot always be the one talking. You also need to be the one who listens. Allow your partner time to express themselves without interruption. Even if your communication styles are different, that respect for each other will help smooth over many misunderstandings.

Go out together. Spend a lot of time together. Be on the lookout for the devil. Call the devil by his name and cast him out. That means praying together, staying together, and sleeping together and not with another. The more you do and share with each other, the stronger the communication, and the more boundless your relationship will become. Your relationship is becoming and processing daily. Remain positive!

Part of the process of spending time together means helping each other to cultivate calm. You can help each other in this regard. If your partner is not on board with the idea, you must still focus on it daily. Take the lead.

You will benefit yourself by letting go of the stress, the anger, and the hurt feelings. When you allow these feelings to build resentment, you are fighting against the calm that is an invaluable part of your life together.

> *"A calm heart gives life to the body, but jealousy is rottenness to the bones."*
> **—Proverbs 14:30**

When you focus on creating calm in your life, it spills over into all your relationships. It helps you find common ground in communication, and you are not so quick to take offense. Part of keeping calm means taking time to think before you speak. Earlier, I spoke about jumping to conclusions and making assumptions and hasty judgment. When you take the time to think before you speak, you are giving love to your partner, avoiding a potential argument in the process, and giving harmony to your union.

Throughout your relationship, you are going to uncover the ways that your partner communicates with you. The question is, are you willing to be open to their communication style and also give them the benefit of the doubt when you are unsure of their meaning? If they love you and you love them, then why would you want to attribute bad intentions or motives to their words? Instead, give them the benefit of loving them first, and allowing mistakes to be just mistakes. Don't compound the mistakes by attributing bad intentions to them and putting your partner on trial as well.

As part of giving and taking, there needs to be a balance so that both partners can feel joy in the giving and the taking. In fact, if you feel as if you are always giving and your partner is always taking, then the communication in the relationship is bound to break down as your resentment and lack of joy grows. It is not always going to be 50/50, but each partner needs to contribute to the upbuilding of the relationship.

Communication is essential and beneficial. However, if you choose to keep account of all injuries and all slights, you are going to find yourself bringing negativity into your relationship. It will take a lot of effort on your part to break negative habits and focus on the positive ones in your relationship. You could even brand yourself Mr./Mrs. Positivity, just to help yourself retain good thoughts about yourself and your relationship with your one true love.

We have all been trained to communicate in specific ways, by our families, friends, experiences, and environments. If you find some areas in your communication style that need attention, make a conscious effort to fix them. Your relationship will improve as a result. Making this effort is not always easy. Therefore, focus on one area of the relationship to remedy at a time, and allow the solution to become your routine. When that effort becomes embedded in your psyche, take on another area that needs attention. Focus on fixing one aspect of the relationship at a time before moving on to fix something else.

Challenge yourself to be open-minded and to see where your partner is coming from by embracing your partner's different perspectives. Building a relationship is not easy. It demands courage—boundless courage— but the benefits are enduring. Simply put, in the end, it is worth all the effort that you put into building up your relationship.

As you have sensed and foreseen by now, communication involves more than just learning and knowing communication styles. It also includes learning the art of compromise. In the next chapter, I will focus on how to incorporate the art of compromise into your relationships, and how compromise can help you and your partner grow together harmoniously.

NOTES

_____

_____

_____

_____

_____

_____

_____

_____

_____

_____

_____

_____

_____

_____

5

The Art of Compromise

5

The beauty of a relationship is that you are enabled to support each other in all situations regardless of what comes your way. The challenge is that it is sometimes hard to support your partner when you do not feel that support in return. The reciprocating feeling is what makes the art of compromise so much more rewarding, because it allows you to find yourself giving up what and where you did not think you could or should.

Plus, there are decisions that come naturally with a partnership. First, you must decide on how you want to demonstrate your commitment to each other, and with your family and your friends as well. Are you going to get married or just live together as partners? And what about children? Will there be any? Then, if getting pregnant becomes complicated, how far are you willing to go to start a family? Would you consider adoption, or would you opt for medical interventions? Medical interventions can be emotionally and financially taxing. Then, when children are born, the question becomes: how will they be raised? Will you both provide all forms of instruction, or will that be the burden of one parent over the other?

These are just a few of the questions that surface as part of a partnership. There will also be questions about where you are going to live, how you are going to manage two careers, and how to manage family finances. This list could go on and on. Each of these questions is going to demand that you both, together, come to some type of agreement. Bear in mind that compromise not only means having to be open-minded and willing to give, give, give. Compromise also means being able to talk through situations and issues, and calculate the risks to yourself, your family, and your community, and then make a logical, smart, and reasonable decision that affects everyone in a positive way.

Throughout these few pages, I want you to not think of compromise as an experience where you must give something up to get something back. Instead, get connected to the reality that the art of compromise is truly about sharing love, and doing so unconditionally, while being at peace with whatever the results or consequences may be. Note, too, that there can be no compromise without conversation.

What Does Compromise Mean?

Compromise is often defined as an agreement or a settlement of a dispute that is reached by each side making concessions. It is an art to balance the desires of both parties, allowing each to walk away feeling that they won the day. In relationships, it is often rarely a simple give and take. There are emotions involved. However, because this is the person you love and have partnered with, it is important to make concessions regardless of your present, temporary, negative feelings toward them at this point. It is not easy to compromise when it feels as though you are being attacked, but true love always concedes to allow peace to reign.

In fact, compromise is not a battle that you must win while giving as little as possible to your partner. Instead, give with an open heart and an open mind to your partner, and the results will blow you away. To work at making your partner happy, creates peace for yourself and strengthens the relationship in the process. It is not always easy, but when you continue to validate your partner, you will find that the joys of the relationship flow back to you.

Not everyone you deal with is going to display this type of attitude, and not every partner is going to be open to giving of themselves in this way. As I will share later, there may be times when you must evaluate the merits of the relationship, and weigh whether it is worth pursuing. In the meantime, let's focus on which elements of the fruit of the spirit can help you to better employ the art of compromise.

If we think of ourselves as mind, body, soul, and spirit, then the spirit aspect of our being is what I want to write briefly about. Galatians 5:22 describes the spirit as a fruit divided into 9 segments: love, joy, peace, patience, kindness, goodness, faith, gentleness, and self-control. When these qualities are present in any relationship, there is also success all round. This is a super guide to managing ourselves and our relationships.

I want to focus on a few of these entities of the spirit as they relate to compromising with our partners. First, let's talk about kindness. When disagreeing with your partner, it is very easy to slip into using unkind words, and to attack their character in an attempt to resolve the issue. However, doing so makes it more difficult to successfully address the problems or challenges you are facing as a couple. On the contrary, being kind to your partner, even during the particularly challenging moments of your relationship, produces very desirable results. The essence of kindness is captured in the words of this poem I learned as a child:

> Kind hearts are the gardens,
> Kind thoughts are the roots,
> Kind seeds are the flowers, and
> Kind deeds are the fruits.

There is a sense of beauty, calm, and peace that flows from the imagery in these words, and this is indeed what relationships need to be able to survive.

Another segment of this fruit is patience. There can be no compromise where there is no patience. It is a virtue that supports and builds compromise. Patience is being able to slow down to think before you act—to weigh your words before giving life to them. It is a vital must-have in every relationship.

As part of an agreement with your partner, you may find yourself giving and waiting for your time to receive. Patience is a quality that helps you to find joy during the wait. No one likes to wait, but patience keeps you from becoming bitter with your partner when the wait gets weightier and you are becoming heartsick over an expectation that has been eternally deferred. However, cultivating and harvesting patience keeps you from becoming sad, jealous, hateful, angry, malicious, and discouraged. Patience cushions you from growing feelings of loss and despair.

Therefore, be patient with your partner. Do not allow small disagreements to grow into divides that threaten the stability of your relationship. As humans, it is common to think in terms of *getting what I want, when I want it*. Practicing patience and being willing to put the needs of someone else first goes contrary to our natural human tendency and ways of thinking. But patience, the ability to wait on others, is virtuous and precious, and beneficial to your relationship.

Whenever you reach an agreement with your partner, regard that agreement with joy. After all, it sours the relationship when you respond negatively to an agreement because not everything went exactly as you would have liked. Bringing joy into the relationship helps you to find peace with whatever comes your way. Challenges help you to grow, and so when you display joy amid a challenge, you demonstrate that you are finding the blessings that naturally result from challenges. Joy is a demonstration of the placement of your focus on the positives rather than on the negatives.

Finally, I want to talk about love. Love is the foundation on which to build a relationship. It is strong, sturdy, and firm. It is not easily shaken. You chose your partner because you admired their beautiful qualities. When you disagree, the strength of your love is being tested, and it is harder to recall that first love. However, love is the binding agent that will help you to keep caring for your partner, to keep giving to them, and to keep trying to do what is best for them and for the relationship. When your partner also tries to see and do what is best for you, you both will benefit positively and tremendously in the end.

Showing love in your responses to your partner also helps you to avoid hurting them by word or by actions. When you are dealing with an area of your relationship where a compromise is necessary, you both will have strong opinions to express. However, your effort and ability to discuss your points of view in a calm and peaceful manner, show love and respect for each other. By not attacking your partner for their opinion or their belief, you are demonstrating love and kindness. Many relationships struggle when both partners focus on being right, at the expense of their unity. This is one way of showing a lack of love during challenging times.

Can you think of ways that you might be struggling to compromise in your relationship? Have you found yourself giving your partner the silent treatment over something you could not agree on? If you give more to the relationship than your partner, do you show resentment? It is important to recognize that how you react when you do not get your way says a lot about character, and can impact your relationship in negative rather than positive ways. So then, let's compromise; let's give some and take some, for the best results.

Highlights of Compromise

Over the years, I have come to think of compromise as also representing some other elements of problem solving within a relationship. Below is my acronym with explanation of how the art of compromise can positively impact your relationship.

C: Creative – When you think about working through a problem or challenge with your partner, the options can often appear very narrow. This is particularly true if both of you are determined to stick to your positions no matter what. When you get creative, however, you start thinking outside of the traditional ways of doing things. In the midst of employing creativity, you may find the solution that gets both you and your partner excited. Do not be willing to stand in your position at the expense of your relationship. Instead, bring creativity to the challenge, and successfully deal with all problems together as a team.

O: Opt Out – When the discussion starts getting heated, opting out gives you both a chance to cool down. Opt out before you get burned, and before both of you say things that you eternally regret. Once words are spoken, they cannot be taken back. Plus, giving yourselves a chance to cool down can allow you to make room for creativity and not for conflict. Opting out gives you the chance to visualize your relationship-building skills. Opting out allows you to see the bigger picture, which is the value and worth of your relationship.

M: Moment – In the moment, you need to be able to recognize when it is time to let go and when it is time to opt out. You can get caught up in the moment without realizing that this is just one moment in your relationship. Do not let that single moment define your relationship in a negative way. Part of understanding the moment is knowing when you need to hop into the discussion, and when it is better for you both to hop out.

P: Peace – Throughout the process of compromising with your partner, try to focus on acting from a place of peace. A calm heart is key to finding solutions. When you get worked up, all you will see is how much you are right, and how much the other person is wrong. Finding the compromise will be difficult if neither of you is willing to bring peace to the situation. If you are looking for what will bring peace, then reaching for unity and calm will make it easier for you both to find the solutions that benefit the relationship. You will not succumb to the stresses and worry of the moment. You are, instead, open to the options that are pleasing, promising, and profitable to your relationship.

R: Restoring – Throughout this process, you want to focus on how you can restore your partner and be refreshing to them. They may be dealing with intense emotions relating to other challenging circumstances as well. If you can work to become a place of refreshment for them, then it will be easier to find solutions instead of giving into the stress and worry of the moment. Restoration puts you in a position to rebuild where necessary. Be open to reaching for the restoring virtues of your challenging situations.

O: Open-Minded – As you deal with challenges in your relationship, it may be easy to focus on what you want. However, that focus can create narrow-mindedness or even closed- mindedness to other options and solutions. Do your best to remain open to hearing what your partner has to say; then reach a place of peace for you both, regardless of the outcome of your argument. Make your partner feel heard and not dismissed. They will be more open to doing the same for you.

M: Making – This part is about making decisions that are upbuilding for your relationship. Strive to build insight into the needs of your partner. What more could you give at this point to address their needs? Finding joy in seeing your partner content and happy helps you deal with the challenges of the relationship, even if you don't end up getting exactly what you wanted. Make yourself emotionally invested in the outcome. In every relationship challenge, one partner is more emotionally invested than the other. Can you choose to give to your partner without resentment, especially at a moment where you are not as emotionally invested as your mate?

I: Intuitive – Working with your partner means being intuitive, sensing why they are unhappy at the moment, even if you don't have evidence to help you understand. This is about tapping into your inner sense to figure out and understand what might really be going on with your partner. When you are intuitive, you ignore the surface actions and reactions because you know that something deeper is at work. You are tapping into your instincts regarding your partner, and using them to guide your choices, words, and actions.

S: Sensitive – At this point, you need to recognize that being logical about a situation could mean hurting your loved one. While you want to share your thoughts about the issue, you need to do so in a way that is sensitive and that takes their feelings into account. That is not always easy to do. However, when you are sensitive to your partner's feelings, your partner does not feel attacked, belittled, neglected, or unwanted, and will in turn strive to become sensitive to your feelings as well. It is a process we must endure, because there are no manuals to guide our progress.

E: Experience – During the process of trying to compromise, bring your experience, as well as your liveliness, to the discussion. Maintain your sense of joy, regardless of the outcome. Remember, you control your reactions to your relationship experiences, and you can make the situation better or worse by your reactions. Maintaining your effervescence is key to having a positive experience overall, so just do it!

Prioritizing the Joy of Your Partner

Traditionally, compromise is seen as a means of giving something in order to get something in return. However, when it comes to truly compromising in a relationship, you may give and the only thing you receive in return is seeing the joy in your partner. There is also the reality that at times you just need to let go of your own ego. If you have a penny, for example, and you give it away, it comes back to you, because you have allowed it room to grow and expand.

Sometimes it is the art of letting go completely and not expecting anything in return that truly benefits your personal well-being and your relationship. In letting go, you allow your relationship to breathe. That is when the good, the beautiful, and the blessings of the bond flow back to you. Think of a grain of corn. When the grain falls into the field, it lets go of all that made it a grain of corn in the first place. This is a demonstration of the true act of letting go. The astounding result is an abundant harvest of corn. If you are holding on and not open to letting go, if you are unwilling to give and take, and if you will not compromise, then you could miss out on great opportunities to reap an abundant harvest of good things from your relationship.

When you let go, your relationship reproduces good that comes back to you in abundance. Letting go does not mean that you have lost. It is a way of planting a seed to receive good returns in the future. Letting go rids you of the stress and frustration, and the bitterness and anger and resentment that spoil your relationship. Harboring negative emotions eats you and consumes you, and leads to horrific acts of violence and death. To let go is to bring peace to yourself and to the relationship. Letting go allows the good of the relationship to come back to you in various, multiple, and incredible ways.

I once made a suggestion to a co-worker; a suggestion I thought was innocent and meant for good. But when I was blasted in front of a crowd, and with the use of some pretty intense and colourful language, I was blown away. Most individuals would have reacted by blasting back. I didn't do that. Instead, I remained calm. Later, I phoned and apologized for what I said that may have been offensive. I didn't ask for an apology. That was not my objective. I was on a search for peace. Yet by letting go of what I felt was my right, I ended up gaining respect, trust, and confidence. Letting go freed me up to live a freer and better life, and allowed me to build a firmer foundation of trust and respect. That's what is desirable for a relationship.

A soft answer does turn away wrath. It allows you to let it go in the moment, and to deal with the matter as soon as possible, when both parties are in a better place emotionally. The best thing is to deal with the matter as soon as you can, because the longer it stays, the harder it gets to reopen and deal with the issue. In relationships, the challenges and irritations that are not addressed promptly can fester and explode. Then as time passes, it becomes harder to heal, or mend or restore the relationship.

There is a strong and urgent need to focus on addressing issues and problems in our relationships. We must, however, be able to resolve them in ways that allow both parties to feel relief and not pressure. With that in mind, I am going to focus on what we should consider when we are dealing with disagreements or other challenges to our relationships.

Wherever there are relationships, there will be disagreements. Disagreements are elemental and foundational to relationship building. It is a fact of life that no two people will always see eye to eye on everything. In fact, you may find that you have real struggles reaching agreements with each other. A disagreement is a call on us to stop, look, listen, and think. It is an awesome opportunity!

After all, challenges have less to do with compromising than with gaining a better understanding of our partners' way of seeing the world. With this in mind, let's race to the next chapter and learn about the right way to argue.

NOTES

_____

_____

_____

_____

_____

_____

_____

_____

_____

_____

_____

_____

_____

_____

NOTES

_____

_____

_____

_____

_____

_____

_____

_____

_____

_____

_____

_____

_____

6

The Right Way to Argue

6

No matter how loving a relationship is, the reality is that there are going to be disagreements and arguments. You are going to have differences of opinion that can lead to conflict between you and your partner. Since arguments are going to happen, it is important that you find a way to argue that allows you to share your opinions and then be open to finding solutions.

One of the first things I want to share is that arguing, or disagreeing, does not have to lead to raised voices and name-calling. When you are starting to attack each other's character or the character of your partner's family, you are effectively shutting down communication. Both parties become defensive, and once the walls go up, the ability to listen and understand goes down, and over time, disappears.

When you are disagreeing with your partner, there is an emotional charge to the situation. You probably feel very strongly about the topic or situation, and so does your partner. How, then, does anyone prepare to face an emotionally charged scenario when in a relationship or before entering one? Let's talk about how to prepare before you enter a relationship. This preparation will help you manage disagreements between you and your partner whenever they happen.

Before you get partnered, recognize that your relationship will be based on two different people coming together, with different cultures, different childhood backgrounds, different experiences, different values, and different points of view. Preparing for your relationship involves learning about your partner, and understanding how relationships work. Doing your homework before you enter a relationship is key to starting off right. There are no magical points of entry. Preparation is key.

Let's think about children. Children represent regeneration and multiplicity. Even in business partnerships, common sense dictates that if your business multiplies, your outcomes are stronger and better. If you decide to start a family relationship but do nothing to prepare for the arrival of children, and nothing to learn how children behave, or what their needs are and how to meet those needs, then you are going to be eternally baffled once they arrive. You'll be even more perplexed when you realize that they have come to stay eternally. It will be even more of a challenge than your twosome relationship already is.

To really be able to manage an argument, you need some training. That training can involve reading on your own, and also practicing how to manage yourself during an argument. In Proverbs, King Solomon wrote that a soft answer turns away wrath. Part of arguing the right way involves exercising self-control. It involves avoiding the use of harsh answers during moments of challenging conversations. Perhaps you spend time with individuals who frequently frustrate you. Practice that soft answer. Make it a habit to answer softly, no matter the situation. It does take practice and effort, especially in those moments when you are emotionally irritated and feeling utterly frustrated.

What can help is to recognize that you cannot control the responses or reactions of the other person, but you can control your own responses and reactions. Too often, people dismiss how important self-control is during a disagreement or when you encounter someone with a different opinion from yours.

I am not saying that you can't feel strongly or passionately about a topic, but I am encouraging you to use self-control when you express yourself during those moments where you are emotionally charged. The suggestion of the soft answer is meant to also remind us that we have a choice to respond rashly and with anger, or to respond softly and with kindness.

If you keep that proverb in your mind, it will help you a great deal with any argument or conversation that poses a challenge for you.

Argue with Your Ears and Your Eyes

The first point I want to make involves changing how you argue by using your ears and eyes. The tendency is to argue first with your mouth. A person may say something that you disagree with, and you immediately feel the need to answer back. Often, the answer that is given back is so hateful that a potentially great relationship is ruined with the beastly words that are spoken.

So then, instead of a lightning bolt answer with the mouth, choose rather to argue with the eyes and ears. Listen to what the other person has to say. Look at them, and try to read what their face and body language are telling you. Then incorporate the principle of the soft answer. The goal is to avoid a hurtful word coming from your mouth, and potentially causing permanent damage to your precious relationship with your beloved partner.

I have found that it helps me to write down the things that my partner is saying. It also helps to let them know that I am writing down what I think I am hearing because it helps me to better understand their point of view and to make sure that I haven't missed anything that they want to tell me. Notetaking should not be used as a weapon against your partner. Use it as a tool to help you to better and more fully hear and understand what your partner has to say. When you make the other person your focus, instead of spending time trying to come up with an on-the-spot defensive response, you are really learning about your partner and coming to a greater understanding of how they feel, think, and express themselves. This takes courage, but it is possible and necessary for the longevity of your relationship.

Slowing down the pace of the discussion can help you to avoid a quick and rash answer that only adds fuel to the fire. One of the ways that I prepare for a discussion is to write down my own viewpoint before the discussion even begins. Writing helps me to better understand my reasoning before the topic even comes up. Now, to be honest, you are not going to be able to predict every argument or discussion. If you know that you and your partner are disagreeing about something, then thinking through your points before the topic comes up for discussion can allow for a smoother and calmer resolution.

People have specific patterns of behavior and their usual ways of reacting to various situations. Sit down and write out how you would respond to a topic or situation you may need to reply to, and practice your responses in front of the mirror. The mirror shows up facial expressions and other body language that help to give meaning to your words.

You may also add another layer of self-analysis by recording and replaying what you sound like while caught up in an argument. The truth is that we often lack the vocabulary to describe for our partners how exactly their words affect us. The result is often a burst of anger massaged by words blasted off like a loaded shotgun. These exercises help you mentally prepare, and allow you to maintain the goal of a soft answer because you prepared before entering a heated moment.

After completing this exercise, you might be shocked by what you wrote down, how you sounded, and what your body language was saying, especially if you have a pattern of responding, to which you have never paid attention. It is often hard to evaluate your responses when you are in the moment. Taking the time to prepare before these situations arise can help you to shift your responses and make them softer and kinder.

When my son entered the seventh grade, I observed a radical transformation in his demeanour, reactions, and responses. That was the place where our family structure had broken beyond repair, and I had moved away with my children. I used all the strategies I knew as a mother to keep us together, but as my son got older, it became apparent that things were not improving; his education was suffering, and my parenting skills were outdated. I desperately sought out a parenting class and found an 8-week long course at McMaster University. I enrolled and attended. I was desperate for answers. It was the insight I achieved through this course that led me to write down what I wanted to say to my child when he made me angry, and when he was uncooperative and insensitive to my needs. I was honestly shocked to see what my thoughts were on paper, and as I reflected on how I would feel or respond if anyone used those words to me, I realised I was not on a path to successfully parent my child.

I realized that if someone were to say those same words to me, I would be angry for the rest of my life. The point of writing is to help you better understand your responses and why people respond to you in a certain way when you say things to them in your customary manner. Often, it is because there is something in your words that is really stinging and hurtful to others, but you might not be aware of it.

Writing something down allows it to stare you right in the face and make you more self- aware. Once you see them and can read them yourself, it gives you the knowledge you need to make better choices and to use different approaches and responses.

Using Silence to Show Your Interest

When your partner is emotionally charged and going off the handle, being silent and allowing them to speak their piece shows that you are there for them. You really want to understand their point of view. If you are interrupting or interjecting every so often, you are not showing interest in what they have to say; you are simply demonstrating that you have a need to be right and to win the debate regardless of the consequences.

Now stop and imagine what might happen if you didn't do that. What if you chose to allow them to speak without any response or interruption from you?

Can you imagine how different the discussion would be? Instead of both of you saying things out of anger, you would be able to have a calmer discussion. Your partner would possibly also be more inclined to let you respond without interruptions once they have finished speaking. If you have been taking notes, then you are able to address their concerns or points without dragging other issues into the discussion.

You are not running away from the problem or issue. Granted, your partner might be looking for you to fire back a response. If they seem angry or emotionally charged because you are not responding, let them know that you are taking time to process. Such a response makes your partner aware that they are valuable to you and are worth your complete attention.

Arguments can go so differently when no one is slamming doors or running away from the discussion in an emotional state. You are there, absorbing the thoughts and feelings of your partner. If you must cry, then it is okay to do so. Allow yourself to be vulnerable with your partner and allow them space to be vulnerable as well.

Do whatever it takes to stay and be there. Allow them to vent uninterruptedly. It might be that you do not respond to them that day or right after they speak. Take the time to process, and to choose the right response to help you resolve the issue. Do nothing to make the situation worse or to create a deeper division between the two of you.

An argument is like a powder keg. You can choose not to ignite it. Try another mode to express yourself. I have mentioned writing several times throughout this chapter, because it works for me. The process allows me to slow down and really think about the issue instead of the emotion surrounding the issue. Solutions come when you opt not to attack each other, but to address the issue instead.

Writing can also help you to see where you are using words that could be hurtful or could cause divisions instead of contributing to a solution or a resolution of the problem. Then you can cross those things out or reword them to make your response more positively productive.

You may even find it helpful to have a close friend read your response and give you their opinion on it. They might be able to help you fine tune your response even further. Also, when you present a written response to your partner, it slows them down, because they must stop and read, then process it before they can respond.

Notice that everything is about slowing down the speed of the discussion, thus allowing everyone to maintain better control over their emotional responses. Your partner might even need to take some time to think about what you have written. You can now open the next phase of your discussion by asking them if they read what you left them, and then get their thoughts. All these steps are meant to allow the emotional fire to die down and to give you both the chance to talk an issue through calmly.

Do not, however, use silence as a closed door. If you see an opportunity to respond without escalating the situation, take advantage of that. You may find that you are not understanding your partner, so ask questions in a tone that shows you are trying to understand and not to attack.

Use silence to allow you to think, to feel, and to allow the other person to express themselves. When you get the opportunity, express your thoughts and feelings, but do so in a respectful way. Bear in mind that this is an important person in your life. You want to show respect for them because you love and care for them. Your goal should never be to hurt them so that you get your way or win the debate.

It is good to be apologetic, especially if your partner is telling you that something you have done is hurting them or causing them pain. We naturally hurt when someone we love is hurting. Pure love will lead you on to do what's right in difficult moments. Love will lead you on to humbly apologize and seek to understand what you did that caused your Love to hurt. You can, then, effectively adjust your actions going forward. After apologizing, remember to ask for the chance to explain your intentions and clear the air.

Even though you still feel or even know assuredly that you are in the right, look for avenues to accept the blame and emphasize that you are not perfect. Take the blame for making mistakes and for misunderstanding your partner. If you look for those opportunities, they will present themselves, and your partner will love and respect your courage. Say what you were thinking, feeling, and imagining. Be open to sharing and expressing what was in your head and heart. There are likely going to be rebuttals, but do not be quick to take offense to those rebuttals. Always remember that the other person also has something to say.

When you say something, expect that the other person is going to respond, and it may not always be in a positive way or even verbally. Remain calm and take notes of all the rebuttals, even if they are not necessarily staying calm themselves. Not all of us are able to think on our feet and snap back with the best responses. Writing will give you time to think about how you are going to reply. Writing will allow you to give calmer responses that are good and uplifting for the relationship. Remember that a soft answer turns away wrath, and a slow answer also helps to diffuse the emotional tension.

Recognize that even if you or your partner says something that hurts, the intentions are rarely to inflict pain. They may be speaking out of hurt or frustration, and it is important to attribute good motives to your partner until it is proven otherwise. Remember to always think the best of your partner; never think the worst. Doing so will make it easier for you to discuss your concerns and to deal with issues at hand.

The point is to use a lot of positives and find out how you can help your partner. For example: "What can I contribute to make the situation improve? What can I do to change the way I am affecting you?" Clearly, the point is to focus on listening, respond calmly with a soft answer, and focus on finding ways to improve, instead of incessantly blaming your partner without taking responsibility for your own actions and responses.

In this chapter, I wanted to focus on how to have discussions and disagreements with your partner without negatively impacting your relationship. Doing so will help your relationship get stronger, and deepen your spiritual connection. There are situations, however, where your partner may be escalating disagreements or using tactics meant to bring you down. In fact, they could be demonstrating a desire to increase their control over you to the point that it becomes dangerous and hurtful. What does courage say in this case?

In the next chapter, the focus on my experiences in an abusive relationship will show you how my courage rebounded. Perhaps you might see yourself in those situations. I also want to share how I was eventually able to walk out of and away from this defunct relationship. Recognize that you must make that closing decision all by yourself, and that there is a variety of ways to find assistance when you need it. Often, the first step to changing an abusive relationship starts by acknowledging the abuse and then reaching out for help. First, I want to talk about some types of abuse, and to highlight the ones that I dealt with during my marriage.

NOTES

_____

_____

_____

_____

_____

_____

_____

_____

_____

_____

_____

_____

_____

7

Is it Abusive?

7

Relationships often have challenges that force you to work tirelessly to maintain them. All these challenges require effort by both parties. The result of doing the work often means that the relationship grows stronger, and the love continues to thrive. However, there are times when the relationship has crossed a line beyond just a few challenges, and requires more than just effort on both sides to repair it. In this chapter, I will identify some of the different types of abuse that could occur in a relationship, and give you some tools to assist you in dealing with the trauma that those situations could bring you.

5 Types of Abuse

Before I start describing the different types of abuse, I want to make it clear that these different types can overlap or be interwoven. Rarely are there instances where just one kind of abuse is experienced in a relationship. Many people struggle to leave an abusive relationship because of these interwoven elements. For instance, someone who is being mentally and financially abused is not likely going to want to struggle to find the resources they need by breaking away, leaving, and starting all over and away from a partner who used to provide that particular form of support.

Sometimes the abuse starts out as mental or emotional abuse, but soon becomes physical as time goes on. There is a pattern of using mental, emotional, and financial abuse to wear down an individual. This wearing away of the psyche makes the individual doubt their own self-worth and personal value, to the point that they believe that they not only caused the abuse but are deserving of it.

Let's begin by taking a look at mental abuse. This kind of abuse is often demonstrated in the way that you are spoken to or referred to by your significant other. They will dishonor and disrespect you. They will call you demeaning names and devalue your self-image on a regular basis. The offender is often kind to you or loving to you on and off from time to time. The objective is to break your spirit and your resilience, and your ability to survive and overcome the challenges of the relationship.

Emotional abuse, on the other hand, is the controlling of another person's actions through verbal and emotional manipulation. This abuse is also referred to as psychological abuse because it is your intangible psyche that is being persistently challenged. Some things to look out for are:

- **Rejection** – Your partner withholds affection or refuses to show affection, either in private or public.

- **Isolation** – Your partner tries to keep you from attending social events, perhaps by staying away with the vehicle or hiding your money and your phone.

- **Terrorizing** – This aspect focuses on threats or some type of punishment, while creating an environment based on fear, where you curtail your behavior to avoid punishment.

- **Ignoring** – Choosing to not speak to you or failing to respond to the behaviors of the other person. In other words, they refuse to acknowledge you at all, and this could be a punishment for displeasing them.

- **Corrupting** – Developing bad habits in you to manipulate you into behaving the way that they want you to. Maladaptive behaviors that fall under this heading could involve aggression, criminal acts, substance abuse, and sexual abuse.

Emotional abuse, however, does not have to be limited to these five entities. It can also occur when one partner is overly critical of the other, either in private or in public. They may use shame tactics or blaming tactics to make you believe that you brought the abuse upon yourself.

Another form of abuse is gaslighting. This is a form of emotional abuse that can cause the victim to question their sanity, their memory of events, and their feelings regarding those events. Your partner may deny that the abuse happened. They may call you crazy, and even accuse you of rewriting history. They may also bring others into the picture while behaving differently and innocently in front of them, to make you feel even more crazy and confused. Their ultimate goal is to make you completely dependent on them, and to compel you to stay in the relationship although it is unhealthy. As a result, you feel obligated to remain with the abusive partner because you are convinced that you are not worthy of anything different or better.

Financial abuse is where your partner takes control of all the finances, and everything related to money, to get you to depend on them for all financial support. No matter what you need, from toiletries to food to clothes and rent, they are going to control all the spending. If they decide to teach you a lesson, that could include leaving you with no money for toiletries, amenities, or food, for days at a time. Financial abuse involves complete control of the money, perhaps making sure that your paycheck goes right into an account without your name on it. And even where there is a joint account, that money may be quickly transferred out so that your access to money is effectively restricted.

Financial abuse also takes the form of using isolation to keep you from holding a job. This limitation guarantees that you are not able to support yourself without your partner. This form of dependency keeps individuals stuck in relationships for an eternity. They are frightened by the vision of hardships brought on by starting over with literally no financial supports.

Physical abuse, on the other hand, involves using violence that creates fear and manipulates you into doing whatever you are told. The shame of being hit or treated violently by your partner, in private or in the public's eye, means that you will go to great lengths to hide the marks of abuse from your social circles and your work circles. The abuser's aim is to keep you in line and fully dependent on them.

Then, there is sexual abuse. Sexual abuse is also known as intimate partner's sexual violence*. This type of abuse involves forcing a partner to have sexual intercourse, regardless of whether they want to or not. Sexual abuse often happens when one partner is under the influence of drugs and is denying the other the right and ability to consent. Sexual abuse rarely happens alone and is not limited to one specific gender or type of sexuality. Often, this type of abuse begins with controlling behavior, and then escalates into more aggressive forms of physical and sexual assault. Sexual abuse can take various forms, not excluding being contracted out to bring in financial

---

* https://www.rainn.org/articles/intimate-partner-sexual-violence

gains to your partner. Whatever form sexual abuse takes, it is important to note that it is wrong. Be on the lookout for it.

All these different types of abuse are focused around creating control, as your partner demeans you, and erodes and destroys your self-confidence in a bid to keep you dependent on them. Abusive manipulation is so strong that you struggle to find the courage and strength to break away, although your gut tells you to get up, walk away, and never look back.

My Journey Through Abuse

During my past marriage, the abuse was primarily emotional, mental, and to a lesser extent, physical. My partner focused on creating control by making me doubt myself, while isolating me from friends and family. One of the ways of controlling me was to make me feel that everything that went wrong was my fault. My ability to smile, the way I walked, the sound of my voice—my very presence was under attack. This blame game gave him a supreme level of power over me while he persisted in constantly planting in my mind that his behavior was my fault. And, amazingly, family, friends, and society at large condone this cruel wrongdoing, and reinforce it by the questions they pose to you to extend the guilt trip on which you have been placed.

If I had done things the way my partner wanted, then he would not have been angry with me, he explained. If I had not been so stupid, then I would have taken care of everything the way he wanted; I would have been able to clean the house and care for him the right way. If something was misplaced or missing, it was my fault. I was called derogatory and demeaning names. I was neglected and disrespected. On one occasion, a police crew, in a fleet of at least 5 cars, showed up in the wee hours of the morning and broke down the front door of my house to make an entrance for him to come in. When I jumped out of bed in my sparsest bed wear to check on the cause of the commotion, I found myself looking down the barrel of a massive shotgun. All this hullabaloo was basically about manipulating me into believing that I was not good enough without him.

When the relationship eventually burst at the seams, some of the things that spilled included infidelity, dishonesty, lack of intimacy, lack of communication, and a loss of sex. There were abundant excuses of having to work nights or to work late hours. There were persistent instances of coming to bed in the wee hours of the morning, wearing belted and buckled blue jeans.

On one occasion, I made a proposal that our family spend the holidays in Mexico or in Cuba. I was interested in the culture and the language. Plus, our children were being exposed to the language in school. It seemed like a good experience for the family. However, this proposal was met with "I have no money," and "I don't know how to spend time with you." His responses left me baffled, dazed, and more confused than ever.

My partner also attempted to manipulate the family situation through our children. He knew what we ought not to expose our children to, yet he would deliberately leave the television on a sex channel. Then when the children came into the house and turned on the television, they would begin where their dad left off. The aim was to hurt me at any cost, even if it had to be through our children. My partner's ability to love any of us was overridden by his deathly desire to control and overpower me.

Consider your partner getting on the phone with other women, in the centre of his wife and children sitting in the living room and watching television. There were times when he would get up and leave the room—bathroom, bedroom, living room, kitchen—if I came into it. I once inadvertently asked, "Are you allergic to me?" It was that weird! At other times, he would just barge into the room, particularly the bathroom, just to make me uncomfortable. Privacy was dictated by him.

At this point in time, I was carrying his second child, which he swore could not be his. This dude burst into the bathroom one day and, on looking at me, exclaimed, "Your belly is so big!" The sum total of the communication between us, during this entire pregnancy, was that put-down statement on the size of my belly. Of course, I was unable to stop my belly from getting progressively bigger so that my partner could become more comfortable with me.

After having made this statement, my partner totally disappeared, leaving me to fend for myself throughout the pregnancy and beyond. I am still caring for this child single-handedly while the father gets off scot-free, or so it seems. This is the kind of mental and emotional aggravation I am referring to. These were the loneliest and darkest moments of my life. I experienced utter abandonment while my partner went off with other partners, leaving me to swim or sink. My partner did not come home at night, did not check in on me, and did not ask how I was feeling or if I needed to see a doctor. There was no care or giving of affection to me during this time. I was lonely, sad, dejected, and mentally and emotionally lost. What should have been an incredibly happy time was a struggle for me to manage my children, and make sure they were cared for. It was also a struggle to even emerge from our dwelling each day to face the world afresh.

Additionally, there were the constant comparisons to other people, particularly other women who were skilled and experienced at a variety of tasks which I did not assume, according to him. I also dealt with the theft of money I earned and saved. That money was meant to pay the hospital bill for the delivery of the baby, and help me to feed the children during my recovery. I had to work to provide the funds to pay the hospital. They would have kept me prisoner unless I paid the bill, so I had to send my partner to the bank for the money. He withdrew the money and paid the bill; then he went back to the bank several times throughout the same day and emptied out my account. There was a consistent lack of support and lack of provisions, not only during the time I was pregnant but throughout the years we were married and living together.

As time went on, I grew increasingly quiet. I had no one to talk to, and there were too few signs of physical abuse. Who would believe me about the things my partner said and did to me behind closed doors? Plus, I highly valued my faith, and I struggled with the standards of the church. The church does not encourage or condone separation, and my standing in the church was also in jeopardy. However, the contacts I had created with others in the community helped me to pull through. I wasn't completely isolated. There were others who reminded me of my self-worth, my value to the community, and my potential for resilience.

Still, I was hurting, but no one could see it because I presented a picture of someone who was managing her life well. Inside, I was falling apart. My laughter was concealing my pain and the psychological destruction that was taking place. I had a profound desire to walk away from this perpetual hell and never look back! What helped me during these dark days were the words from the song, "One More Valley," where it says:

Don't let Satan see your tears.

Learn to smile through those fears.

Hold your head up high and give the world a smile,

You must be faithful all the way,

Twill be worth it all someday,

For it's all gonna be over after a while.

Surprisingly enough, most abusers may have dealt with abuse in their own lives. They carry around feelings of not being good enough, and now they want to control another person in order to deal with their feelings and insecurities. However, this just perpetuates the cycle of abuse, and the victim must decide whether or not to stick with the relationship, or when, where, why, or how to get out of it.

Challenges Continue to Grow

I tried to talk with my partner and to discourage the behaviors that were setting the children against each other. (Our son was openly favored over our daughter.)

However, my urgings fell on deaf ears. It was like talking to a brick wall. That unwavering determination to spend money and time on our son alone meant that he also denied medical care to our daughter when she desperately needed it. This determination to treat our daughter as inferior left her not willing to talk with her dad to this day. She refers to him as a sperm donor, and her outlook on men in general is decisively clouded by the treatment dished out to her by her dad. In my partner's deathly determination to control me, he has also ruined his relationship, not only with his daughter but also with both his children, as neither of them will talk to him now.

My choice to remain in the relationship, and to try all in my power to make it right, came from growing up in the church. The teachings are opposed to separation and divorce. Additionally, I wanted a second child and did not want to have two different fathers for my children. However, I arrived at a place where I was completely ready to give it all up. My mother was vaguely supportive. She did not encourage me to leave but hinted at what supports she could offer. The day I decided to pack up and leave, my partner decided to talk. Then he apologized and made copious promises that it would be different. However, no sooner had I agreed to stay in the relationship, than my partner returned to his old behaviors. Nothing really changed.

When you are trying to decide whether you are going to stay or leave, your partner may try to convince you to stay. They may promise the moon, offer to get counseling, and also tell you that they didn't mean anything they had said or done in the past. It was all a joke, and they thought you knew they were joking. What is clear is that actions speak louder than words. It is rare for abusive partners to follow through on their promises.

I sought out counseling without my partner. He wanted nothing. I wanted solutions. I wanted the relationship. As you might figure, however, it was a one-sided situation. No relationship can be mended with only one of the members looking for change and for amends. While counseling was helping me to get my head on straight, allowing me to build up my courage to finally make a change, my partner was stuck in a determination to have his cake and eat it. So, after two decades of dealing with this situation, I paid to talk with a lawyer who told me what I could and could not do if I chose to break away. In the end, the lawyer told me that I needed to go with my gut feelings and to decide what was best for me and for the children.

Eventually, I realized that I could not keep talking to people about my situation. I had been talking for 20 years now. I needed to make a decision and to stick with it. The day came that I decided I was ready to leave. However, those who had promised to help me at this moment of decision were suddenly unavailable. I was not deterred. There was a lesson in this for my daughter, and also for my son. I needed to do this for myself and for my children. And hopefully, my partner could wake up to a thing or two. This invaluable move depended on a crucial decision I must make; and though it was out of character, I could not rob my family and all of humanity of this lesson that needed to be taught and learned.

So, after spending the night at my mother's, and leaving the children at school the following day, I went to the house alone and set about packing. When the children got home, they asked, "Mommy, what are you doing?" I was too busy and too engrossed to hear it, so they got the silent treatment. I knew that if I started conversing, it would distract me from the task at hand. When they saw there was no forthcoming answer, they declared, "You're not leaving us," and with that, they got out their suitcases and started packing their stuff to follow wherever their mother went. One thing that helped me make this move was what the lawyer said: "Follow your gut feeling." Know that there is a voice in your gut that's constantly speaking to you.

While all this transpired, my partner sat at the table, playing on his phone and straightening his nose, while his family packed and prepared to leave. In the meantime, the moving truck I had arranged showed up as soon as my partner left with the family car to go on another of his lovers' trysts. I have heard many stories of partners moving out and taking all, but I did not clean out the house as per the lawyer's advice.

When we lived together, I paid the rent, and he was supposed to provide food and pay the bills. Food for him was fast food. I was not given the money to shop for healthy foods, and any sign of healthy food would soon disappear from the house. The children and I were literally starving. Once I moved out, though, our need for food was miraculously and abundantly met, mainly by new friends and some family too. We had so much that I was able to share with my new neighbours. My children and I were being cared for, and I felt the blessings of God, our provider and way-maker, for the decision to move out and on.

It is up to the individual when or if you decide to leave. It is important for you to listen to the voice in your gut and to also make a plan. Faith and trust in God can give you the courage to make the decision to leave, and follow through with that decision, if you must. Keep in mind, only you can decide when it is time to go. It is your gut that will talk to you. Your country or state may also offer resources for those leaving abusive relationships. Do not hesitate to ask for help. When you do, it can build you up to stay the course. There may be moments when you wonder whether you made the right decision. Just remember that the voice in your gut is never wrong.

The opportunity to migrate came soon after, as on the death of my father, one of my aunts discovered the degradation under which I lived, and offered to help me make my way to Canada. Everything was done and complete, and when it was time to leave for Canada, my partner made a written declaration of an inability to travel with his family.

I was so excited because that meant we were free to start a new life. The government gave him an extension to travel on the visa I had obtained for him, but he disregarded that time frame. Now the children and I are in Canada, and with that distance, I was able to start building life afresh for myself and my children, without the sabotage and abuse of the relationship.

However, although I was physically free, I still had to file for divorce, which took 14 years, plus a fortune, to complete the process. For me, processing the divorce was like reliving the abuse from another angle. This experience added to my scare of entering another relationship. I felt I wasted the better part of my life through this relationship.

You may find that after leaving an abusive relationship, a reluctance to get into another relationship sets in. For me, the reason I got married was to have children. I had my heart fixed on four. My partner wanted one, plus a jolly play-house time. Now that I have had two children, I feel satisfied to have gained some learning in this regard, and do not need to yearn for more. In fact, our government taught us that two is better than too many, and I have come to value that teaching above my desire. Remember, leaving an abusive relationship is just the beginning. So, consider counseling to help you deal with the trauma, and be aware that you are going to do things in your own time.

There are also the side effects of trauma on your children. My son witnessed his father being physically violent to me, and later, when at 13, he also got violent with me. This is the mystery of how we learn. You tell me, and I forget. You show me, and the memory is everlasting. I realized this when my son admitted that he had seen his father hit his mother. There are long-term consequences for the children, so it is important to find resources to help them address their own traumatic experiences as soon as possible after leaving the abusive household.

If you are dealing with this type of experience, be open to finding help. Reach out and get help. Building connections can help you to see that this is not about you, but it is about the abuser and their desire to be in control at your expense. Once you leave, do not look back. Looking back is a form of suicide. Push forward. Push ahead. It won't be smooth sailing, but be courageous. If you push ahead, you will find the calm that you deserve. You deserve to be safe.

Now that I have talked about abusive relationships, I want to be clear that not every relationship is abusive. Instead, you could be faced with situations stemming from a lack of communication or a loss of intimacy. The question is: how can you ride out these challenges and save your relationship? Let's rush to the next chapter, where we will explore some challenge-related strategies.

NOTES

_____

_____

_____

_____

_____

_____

_____

_____

_____

_____

_____

_____

NOTES

8

Riding the Storm to Save
Your Relationship

8

This chapter is about preparing for and managing Dorian, the category five and above relationship challenges you will face. In the islands, hurricanes are a frequent occurrence. When it is hurricane season, our regular routine includes battening down the hatches, and preparing for the storm to hit land. Storms always bring a great deal of wind and rain, which causes plenty of damage and loss of life.

Individuals and families focus on limiting the damage and preventing loss of life. They put protective and preventative measures in place before the storm begins. They also affix hurricane shutters, gather food and water, and move to higher ground.

When you hit upon storms in your relationship, how well you make it through is based on the preparations that you made in advance. What are some of the ways that you can prepare your relationship to weather the storms of life?

What Types of Storms are There?

No matter how long you have been in a relationship, there are still going to be storms that occur. These storms can be a source of growth for your relationship, or they can batter your relationship to the point that it simply cannot survive. Here are just a few of those storms and what they might look like in a relationship.

Misunderstandings

We might think that our communication skills are off the charts, while our partners vehemently disagree. The truth is that misunderstandings between partners occur all the time, and we often attribute intentions to our partners that are judgmental and not at all true. Consequently, how we hear what our partners say is often filtered through the intentions we assign to them. Other misunderstandings are based on expectations related to what we thought we heard, against what was really said or intended.

When misunderstandings fester, they become a divide between two individuals. Like literal storms, the trickle of a misunderstanding turns into a flood of resentment. The damage that flooding causes often destroys everything that you built together over a long relationship.

Emotional Abuse

Those who have dealt with emotional abuse understand the toll that it can take. These abusive winds can whip around you and cause severe distress and damage. Over time, if winds of emotional abuse persist and continue, the damage becomes overwhelming, and the trust and love that once held the relationship together are affected beyond repair.

Financial Abuse

For couples dealing with financial abuse, the experience can be likened to a form of flooding, one that takes time to build and gather momentum before wreaking havoc in the relationship. One spouse may be completely out of the loop regarding what the other is spending or doing with their finances. Months or years later, they may find out that debt is now mounting, and what they had worked for all their lives is now crumbling or gone. The emotional hurt, and damage done to the trust, effectively wreck the very foundation of the relationship. As the saying goes, "No money, no love." Love and money are so intertwined that it is hard to care about one and neglect the other.

Poor Communication or Vague Wording

This communication storm, where one partner is never being clear or precise about what they mean, can batter a relationship for years on end. A lot is left to the imagination and is often incorrectly interpreted and, often too, there is no forthcoming clarification. I am presently working with a partner whose utterances consistently leave me with many questions. However, when given a chance to clarify, my partner freezes and bluntly refuses to answer. I am left to think of myself as being slow of understanding, or maybe outrightly daft.

Using passive aggressive communication styles, or simply vague wording, often leaves a partner thinking or understanding one thing, when their mate means something different. Do not get me wrong; this is not a blame game. It is an attempt to bring to light some realities that negatively impact relationships that are otherwise perfect. This kind of storm reflects a deep-seated problem that may have been brought on through child-rearing practices or through elements in the environment where your partner grew up. The good news is that these character defects are not rare, and can be resolved through intervention strategies.

When the storm of poor communication is insidious and deliberate, when it results from spite or strife, when it is driven by hurt feelings, it becomes more damaging and can lead to violence and death. If it becomes impossible to resolve a storm of this nature, think quickly, weigh your options, and make the safest choice of staying or leaving the bond. The storm of poor communication can be life threatening.

Arguments

While arguing fairly can help you to clear the air with your partner, the truth is that arguments filled with personal attacks can tear down your partner and devastate your relationship. This storm is full of lightning and thunder and strong winds of malice and strife. These bitter winds inflict emotional and mental destruction. Ultimately, your partner feels undervalued, worthless, dejected, unwanted, and hopeless as the attacks increase and the emotional divide grows and flourishes.

The Obstacles of Life

Then there is the storm called life, packaged in sickness, financial difficulties, and troubles of every type that can bombard a relationship. During these storms, you both need to rely on each other even more, though this may be difficult or even impossible to do. By taking the time to shore up your relationship before the storm, and then continuing to connect with each other during the storm, your relationship will stand the test of time.

Clearly, there are many storms out there, some still waiting to be born, and you may have already encountered some of them. The question we must answer, though, is how to prepare for these storms, and how to manage them when they hit. Our objective is to fortify our relationship so that it not only survives, but that it thrives.

Look for the Potential Weaknesses

As you and your partner spend time together, you will notice distinctive patterns of dealing with each other. There will be the specific ways your partner communicates, and other habits that positively impact the relationship. Before the storm hits, be on your double guard by always looking out for potential weak areas, and then reinforce them with love, patience, kindness, gentleness, peace, and as many other positive qualities that make a relationship stand the test of time. Before a storm hits is the best time to evaluate the state of your "house," and to determine where reinforcements are needed.

Throughout this book, I have shared information about various challenges or areas of concern that might creep into our relationships. Most of these challenges are based on communication and how well each party supports the other. At the point where it all appears to be smooth sailing, when it is the calm before the storm, take note of how you communicate with each other.

- Do either one of you tend to go silent or ignore the other if their feelings are hurt?

- Does communication simply stop if there has been a misunderstanding or blunt discussion?

- Do you find yourself holding onto grudges over relatively small things?

- Do you apologize to each other?

- Do you spend time every day doing something for the other person, just to make them feel loved, appreciated, and thought about?

- Do you make time to listen to each other without the distractions of electronics?

- Do you regularly make time to spend together doing something you both enjoy?

- Do you actively look for ways to learn more about your partner, so that you deepen your relationship?

Ask yourself these questions, because if you or your partner negatively exhibit any of these habits while the waters are calm, then those behaviors that are negative, essentially become the weaknesses that destroy your relationship during the storm. I am not saying that you can't survive the storm with unattended weaknesses; however, the resulting damage to your relationship could take years or forever to make right again.

I encourage you to evaluate your relationship with a critical eye. The goal of this evaluation is not to tear down your partner, but to help you look for ways to build each other up, to sensitize you to what needs adjusting, and to support you in fortifying the relationship against all storms.

Here are some key tools to use as part of your kit for strengthening and reinforcing your relationship:

- **Speak Up** – Don't let things fester in your heart. Bring them out in the open, but do so in a calm manner. Talk with your partner during a quiet time when you both can share what is in your hearts. Do not use it as a time to attack, but as a time to share and learn. When you take the time to speak up, you are helping your partner understand you better, and you can clear the air by getting things off your mind. Plus, the concerns and misunderstandings that you have can now be dealt with, instead of being left unanswered and allowed to become the cause of damage to an otherwise great relationship.

- **Listen Up** – While it is important for you to be heard, it is equally important to listen to your partner. Remember, your partner wants to be heard too, and for this to happen, someone must be listening. Listening up is about giving your mate a safe space to be heard and understood. Do not be quick to interrupt, but instead be open to listening without trying to formulate a rebuttal in the moment. Be open-minded as you listen, and don't make snap judgments about your partner's intentions. It will surprise you how much you learn about your partner when you spend time listening.

Throughout this process of building up your relationship, it is important to never go silent. If you do, then when storms hit, your silence could isolate you from the support of your partner. If you are sad or mad, it is important to speak up and let someone know what is going on. Keeping things inside never benefits your relationship, particularly when you are hit by the different storms I mentioned before.

Another useful tool is to *Suck it Up* and make yourself visible to your partner. Never hide away! Hiding away does not make the problems go away. Hiding away allows time for more damage to be done to your relationship. Also, maintain calm during the discussions. Being calm helps you to see more clearly where you need to change in order to be a better partner. In a relationship, no one is without fault; but if you are fully focused on the wrongs of your partner, you can miss recognizing how you yourself are contributing to the weak areas in the union.

Being calm involves being open to learning and receiving honest feedback about how you can do better. It means being enabled to see how and where you failed. It means taking that information in so that you can learn and grow. In the writings of King Solomon, the wise, are the words: "By humility and the fear of the Lord are riches and honor and life." Humility is another way of expressing a state of calm. To be calm is not being weak.

It is a place of strength that produces wealth, respect, and the status which we all desire.

If you exercise calm in working with your partner, before, during, and after a storm, then you are honoring your partner and their place in your life. To have good things come into your relationship, there needs to be an opening to learn while going through difficulties. Tough times are better endured and overcome together, and then what you want as an individual and as a unit, will come to you in the end.

Be Honest with Your Partner

It is also very critical to be honest with your partner. While some of the concerns and issues that you have might cause temporary hurt feelings, ignoring them to avoid causing hurt could create more harm than good. A mild answer can turn away rage, but mild should not mean dishonest.

Calmly express yourself at a time when both of you are open to listening. Don't try to have an honest conversation when you are both heated up. When you are angry, your conversation quickly turns into a non-productive argument. That is when you and your partner eventually say things that are hurtful to each other, and that you both very soon regret.

Also, be alert to signs that things may not be going well with your partner. Don't hide your head and get yourself so busy with other things that you miss key signs that a storm is brewing. Those who live on the islands know the signs of an impending storm, and they do their best to prepare for it in advance. Others who ignore the signals and signs of the storm put their lives and their property at risk. Do not put your relationship at risk by burying your head in the sand or by ignoring the signs that are loudly saying something is not right. Get into action right away. Do something about it if you value the relationship.

The key is that there is always something or someone seeking to dismantle or destroy your good relationship. Keep your feelers out, be on the alert, become sensitized to the fact that something, some invisible entity, is always trying to break you. Are you going to ride it out by being prepared, or will you run away and hide? You must work consistently to strengthen and deepen your relationship with your partner to be able to weather whatever storm might come your way. Place a hedge of protection around your bond, if you believe it is worth preserving.

Be open to various strategies that can help to strengthen your relationship. Some individuals use prayer, others build a routine to create and spend quality time with their partner. The point is to find what works for you and then implement those strategies. Believe me, relationships are worth the hassle. It can become easy to give up just when the storm is about to break, so do whatever works to keep your relationship strong, and avoid giving up. Don't just rely on the fact that things have been good in the past. Work to keep them good, and get them better. The superlative, *best*, is always desirable. The effort to protect and maintain your relationship is worth it, so continue to work together to strengthen your connection with each other.

Wise Up is another key strategy to attend to. It involves being proactive. Inform yourself about ways to strengthen your relationship. Read about and implement strategies with your partner to fortify your relationship. Use counseling to help you improve your communication, especially during those periods of time when you think everything is fine. Having a mindset for constant improvement will allow you to avoid taking your partner and your relationship for granted. Build a bank of knowledge that can help you understand how your partner thinks and how they view life. Use that knowledge to guide you as you polish and build the relationship into what you really desire.

Build Up is an approach that allows you to create a community of individuals who keep encouraging you to fortify and build your relationship. Sharing stories with each other is one way of brainstorming strategies that can help you in ways you did not even realize. Many of the thoughts that you do not share with others, you may find are mirrored in other stories and cultures. These strategies will give you insight into changes you might need to make, and about things you can do to transform your relationship into what you want it to be.

Open Up means "No man is an island," so share, share, share. Do not try to fight the storms on your own. Consider counseling during the storm, and tap into other available resources to help you grow your relationship. Talk with older, more experienced couples who have dealt with storms all their lives. Listen and note what they have done to keep their lives together and their relationship glowing strong and bright. Then practice some of those relationship styles, and keep the ones that work best for you. Remember, relationship building is a lifelong process, and one of the keys that can't be overlooked is *communication*. So, share all your new knowledge with your spouse; and together, agree upon a plan of action before implementation. Never, and I repeat, *never* assume it is okay to do things on your own. Always get an input from your spouse or partner.

Finally, think, act, and live to *Love Up*. The *love up* strategy allows you to tap into the care that you truly have for each other. Use it as the foundation to keep your relationship intact during any storm that may arise. Often, when things are at their worst, this is when you need to love on each other even more! No matter what is happening, give love and lift each other up. Every opportunity that you get to build up your partner, to say something encouraging, to acknowledge the things that they do for you, and to fertilize and invigorate their love for you, take advantage of it. This will lift your relationship up and not push it down.

When troubles come, you will be able to survive them and even thrive in the middle of the storms, because you prepared in advance, and you took steps to manage the possible effects of battering and devastation before the onset. Still, some storms will wreak more havoc than you anticipated. Extramarital affairs and abuse of all kinds can do significant damage to your relationship. However, if you decide to rebuild the relationship after the storm has passed, race to the next chapter for ideas on recapturing and rebuilding the love and trust you shared at the start of your life together.

NOTES

_____

_____

_____

_____

_____

_____

_____

_____

_____

_____

_____

_____

_____

NOTES

_____

_____

_____

_____

_____

_____

_____

_____

_____

_____

_____

_____

_____

9

Rebuilding Your Relationship After Overcoming Obstacles

9

No matter what the challenges or storms a relationship encounters, there will be moments where one must make a conscious decision to continue or to abandon the relationship. Many of the storms you face in a relationship will cause a great deal of stress, will potentially hurt your feelings, and may even damage your trust. That is the reason the journey through this book focuses on identifying the various relationship challenges, and provides you with tools to positively confront them.

This chapter is dedicated to those who are choosing to opt into the relationship; those who are not at all opting out. To repair and rebuild a relationship requires complete dedication to the process. Therefore, do not hold one foot out the door, on the off chance that it is not going to work. The doubtful Thomas approach is a sure guarantee for a broken, shipwrecked, ceasing-to-exist relationship, with no progress and no hope of repairing it.

Relationship storms, be they the category 5 winds and rain of infidelity or abuse, may have hurt you so deeply that you now find yourself dealing with the aftermath of horrific damage to the trust and honesty you once had. Your intimacy and connection are also hanging on by a meagre thread. In these moments, many partners struggle to decide whether it is worth it to stick together, or to opt for the seemingly easier route of simply separating and being over and done with it. If your relationship struggles have brought you into the eye of the storm, and have caused you extensive damage in the destructive path, then it is time to take decisive action to rebuild or to totally annihilate the relationship.

Determining whether you can move forward in the relationship depends on how you both respond to the idea of continuing to stay together. Do you both want to stick together? Are both of you trying to repair the relationship? If so, then you can survive this storm and move forward together. Begin by summing up the value of being together, and examining whether there is room for value to be added.

It is not easy to move forward after the storm has passed. There will be focused, emotional work to be dealt with as both of you commit to making changes that will rebuild, refashion, and reshape the damaged relationship into a working relationship. This process demands time and concerted effort, as well as the inclusion of a third party, as you work on approaching each other differently. Your focus must now be on how you can strengthen your connections with each other and deepen that intimacy of the relationship.

When a storm passes through the islands, we engage in an initial assessment of the damage that was caused. Then we put a plan in place to clean up and make repairs. Try to now focus on this process, which mirrors the psychological and emotional experiences in your relationship. Recognize that this storm—this challenge to your relationship—has passed, and it is time to reflect and assess, and determine together what damage was done, and where you need to clean up, rebuild, and repair to shore up your relationship. Let's face it; a relationship can drag on forever if there is never a shaking that forces a change. So, storms are not all bad. Their purpose is to create renewal and bring rewards to the survivors. In high school, the words that helped us succeed were: "Life is the battle of the survival of the fittest." These words have helped me survive in the most despairing situations. If you survive one relationship storm, you are classified among "the fittest."

Thinking of crops, our best products are reaped always after a storm has passed through and wreaked havoc, but leaves in its wake a rich deposit of plant food and nutrients that cannot be bought off the shelves of a store. In the same manner, the storms of living together bring us disruption and turmoil, but they also bring us deposits of a greater understanding of each other and of human nature. They leave us in wonder and amazement, and allow us an opportunity to employ compassion, care, and boundless love, so that we get the best out of our need to live and to share ourselves with someone else.

First Things First, Communication

Let's start with the most obvious thing to get the clean-up process moving. That involves finding a calm and quiet time where you can both sit down and share with each other. I cannot stress enough how important it is to listen with an open mind and an open heart. The storms would have caused devastating emotional damage, and that makes it easy to listen from a place of hurt. However, to listen from that place means closing your mind to what your partner is saying. It also allows you to attribute negative intentions to your partner's actions.

On the other hand, to consciously put your hurt feelings aside, and to listen with an open mind, will allow you to hear your partner's sincere desire to make changes, to repair the relationship, and to grow with you into the future. Listening with an open mind allows you to arrest the spirit of sincerity that keeps rash decisions at bay.

When you build a new house, you take it one element at a time. The process takes time and patience, and at times, it means having to take away some elements to be able to reshape the house to fit your needs. Like building a house, a relationship that has experienced intense challenges will need time and patience to rebuild, reshape, reform, and to create the type of relationship that both of you desire and need.

It is a lifetime of constantly cleaning and polishing and refining your relationship to make it the best that it can be. No matter who you are or what you and your partner have overcome, you cannot ever assume that there is nothing left that can be improved. Growth and healing in a relationship starts by recognizing the importance of service, and the power of gratitude and giving. You cannot, however, know what your partner needs or how you can best serve them if you do not open your ears and heart to tune into their needs.

The rebuilding process is not easy. It is real determined hard work. This is a time to be selective and to choose what to keep and what to discard. You will also want to be careful not to discard anything of value. To be successful at repairing the relationship, you must be very serious but pliable about the process, while bearing in mind what you want to get out of the relationship. If you put in extra love, you will get love out of it. The same is true if you put in extra care. You will get care coming back to you. This principle is very critical when you are both working to clean up, to rebuild, and to repair and restore your relationship.

Increasing Awareness and Gathering Your Building Blocks

One of the results of coming out of a stormy relationship is that your intuitive vision has cleared and sharpened. You are now much more aware of your surroundings, of where your relationship stands, and what the possibilities for the future together can be. This is your plateau moment where you can jointly rest, view, review, and strategize your move forward. There might not be much to your building right now, but by making the decision to stay together and work through the kinks, it allows you to stand with your partner on solid ground.

As part of your increasing intuitive awareness and vision, you and your partner can now review Chapter eight and all the different tools included there. You will find that much of your rebuilding and repairing process is going to involve becoming aware of all existing counter-productive habits, so that you can work on clearing them away together. You are learning where you both stand now, and where you want to go next.

All the negatives that were in place before are what you both have now decided to put behind. It is time to refocus your efforts on rebuilding the broken walls, by putting thoughtfully chosen building blocks in place to help you protect and rebuild the relationship. It will help you to make a physical list of those elements that heightened your awareness of how best to secure and protect your relationship going forward. The intimacy of pen and paper helps to foster enduring memory, which is very valuable for building the foundation of your own relationship.

The very first element to list is love. The pure, sincere love you have for your partner will help you overlook minor offenses and make the effort to forgive the bigger infractions. When the scriptures talk about love covering a multitude of sins, it helps us understand how love can positively impact our relationships. We all make mistakes in our relationships. None of us is infallible. No one is blameless. Therefore, when we want our partner to overlook our mistakes with love, we need to do the same for them. So, as we push for peace in our relationships, we find we must consciously and intentionally forgive our partner's mistakes so that the joys of being forgiven can flow back to us. Whatever you deem this principle to be — karma, reciprocity, or retribution — the fact remains that when the seeds of love are sown, they abundantly reproduce more seeds of love.

In the love book of the Bible, 1 Corinthians 13, many attributes of love are discussed. These attributes function as building blocks to help the growth and protection of any relationship. The first aspect of love mentioned in this chapter is patience. When you are relating to your partner and are facing a frustrating situation, it can be easy to snap off and release your first response of irritation that comes out. On the other hand, being patient with yourself, and with your partner, provides you the means to avoid speaking rashly and angrily, but rather lovingly and softly. Now both can speak clearly and respectfully to each other, without causing hurt or shame, because patience was exercised.

Another attribute of love is kindness. Take time to be kind to your partner in many different ways, because doing so gives you the opportunity to build up the relationship. Kindness often takes very little effort on our part, yet our partner feels loved and appreciated by those very simple, caring gestures.

Take a few minutes to think of a few kind deeds that you can do for your partner. They do not have to be large efforts, but simple things that could be done throughout the day. By adding kindness to your daily routine, both of you benefit, and your relationship is strengthened. Think of the last time you did something kind for someone. Didn't it warm your own heart to see the joy on their face because you took the time to think of them?

Imagine the impact that a show of kindness could have on your partner, who is the closest person to you. Every time you make the effort to be kind to them, it brings you both a bond of joy and love. The show of kindness is a way of drawing individuals closer together and also of deepening their bond. Clearly, it is worth the effort to show your partner how much you care about your union, through the efforts you make to be kind.

Another key relationship building block is unselfishness. With unselfishness, you are not looking out for your own individual, personal self-interests, but for the interests of the bond. I find this building block particularly interesting for couples who are working to repair and rebuild their relationship. When you are focused solely on your own self-interests and what you want to get out of the relationship, you are not likely to do things in the interest of your partnership. You will not be inclined to sacrifice anything for your partner's well-being. That type of relationship will not last, because it is built on selfishness rather than on love. Now, imagine if you take the time to look out for the interests of your partner, even if it means making a sacrifice; those efforts will help your partner to see how important they are to you, and that will draw you both closer together.

All these suggestions are meant to help you focus on giving to your relationship without selfishly focusing on your own interests and needs at the expense of your partner's needs. Many relationships cannot be repaired after a major storm, because both partners want to focus on having their own needs met. In this way, a partner essentially takes from the relationship without giving anything in return.

One of the greatest gifts that you can give your partner is your forgiveness. Think of all the times throughout the day when your partner may have said or done something without being mindful of your feelings. Then think about how many times in the same day that you may have done the same to your partner—not deliberately, of course, but because it is the human tendency to make mistakes. When you opt to not keep account of the injury, but instead choose to forgive, you are showing a deeper love for your partner. Having a heart of forgiveness can smooth over many of the small irritations of life. However, forgiveness also needs to play a part in healing the hurt from infidelity and other storms within your relationship.

What is forgiveness? Forgiveness is, essentially, letting go of the resentment and hurt feelings relating to those negative, painful events experienced, and choosing not to carry them around or carry them forward with you forever. You and your partner will need to discuss those events and plan to resolve them as they arise. Only the individual can choose to let go of resentment toward another person. Letting go becomes easier if you can see your partner with the same eyes you would use to view your beloved sister or brother. Becoming "one flesh" is synonymous with "having the same blood." There is no flesh without blood. If you can find the place of compromise for your brother or sister, it is even more possible to find it for your partner. Compromising leads to forgiving, and forgiving helps your relationship to repair and rebuild, no matter how intense your storms may have been.

Throughout the chapters in this book, I have focused on the need of both partners to show a willingness to give and to forgive. When both parties are focused on giving to the other, it is amazing how easily each of your individual needs are met.

Building Endurance and Hope

Every storm that you and your partner successfully deal with helps to strengthen your bond with one another. Storms build endurance, and endurance allows you to continue to remain firmly committed to the relationship whenever fierce and challenging situations and experiences arise. Clearly, relationships are synonymous with storms, and storms, by nature, are for wearing down the love and trust you have built for one another. Having an awareness of this factor does not only help you to prepare to meet your challenges, but also to build that endurance that is needed for you to block that eminent destruction of your relationship's love and trust.

If your relationship has been rocked by infidelity, you may find it challenging to believe your partner or to trust what they have to say. However, at some point, it becomes needful to allow your love for your partner to help you to trust them. Then, instead of second guessing or trying to figure out if they are telling the truth, allow your love to build your belief and trust in them. Provide them with an abundance of positive feedback, and intentionally refuse to focus on the negatives. It is not always easy to manage the downplay of negatives, but your sincere love will help you to grow in this area of your relationship. On the other hand, being jealous will bombard your love, and blindside you so you cannot move past your relationship storms and into the clean-up phase. Clean up is critical after a storm, so it is important to keep jealousy at bay by focusing on what is good, positive, and uplifting about your relationship.

What practical steps can you take to help you deal with your jealousy? First, write down the reasons you feel jealous, and the circumstances that can trigger it. Share these things with your partner in a calm and quiet manner. Speak from the heart, but without attacking your partner's character. Instead, share how you feel, and allow both of you to come up with solutions to help yourselves manage jealousy. Also, write down the solutions. This will help you to deepen your relationship with each other, as you both work to repair and rebuild it.

Love is also essential for building up hope in the future of your relationship. Allow your love for your partner to keep you looking for your partner's good qualities. Focus on what were your first attractions, and look for, expect, and hope for positive outcomes. Hope, as an optimistic state of mind, is highly desirable in this experience, because when hope is coupled with love, love feeds off hope, and hope strengthens love in return.

The hope that your relationship will last is enforced by your positive conversations and interactions with each other. Pay attention to and write down all the ways that love can benefit your relationship. You will begin to see how important it is to cultivate a deeper love for your mate.

While these last two chapters have focused on building up and rebuilding your relationship, the next chapter is going to deal with how to manage ending a relationship. If after you have tried every avenue humanly possible to save your relationship, you find that your efforts are all futile, then it may be time to leave the union. Leaving must, however, be done so that your interests are protected, to allow you to continue to live in a way that is humane and true to who you are.

NOTES

_____

_____

_____

_____

_____

_____

_____

_____

_____

_____

_____

_____

_____

10

When All Else Fails

10

Appreciating that a relationship has reached its end is never easy. After years of being together, divorce is very painful. A variety of factors would have contributed to the ending of the relationship. Abuse of various types and infidelity are two of the main catalysts to this very stressful experience. The decision to end the relationship is not only challenging but involves serious work and time commitment.

At this point, you would have accumulated the trappings of a life together. There are now assets to be divided, custody over children, and determining how any debts are to be shared or dissolved. While all these discussions are going on, it can be easy for your emotions to dominate and control your actions. Arguments and disagreements often result as the situation gets more and more heated. The atmosphere is now fertile and conducive for you both to hurt each other even further. In fact, whereas there may not have been any previous bodily damage, the climate is now charged and ready for physical combat.

Below are some ways to help you better manage the ending of your relationship. While it is still an emotionally painful process, you can manage it so that you are not left wallowing in the mud when all is said and done.

Be Open-Minded and Listen

Your assets will be a main bone of contention. Perhaps your now defunct partner is trying to take something only because you have an emotional attachment to it. You both may be attached to things and must decide who gets what. This can be challenging. Before you allow yourself to stubbornly fight for your "rights," open your heart and mind to listen to what your bygone partner has to say. You may be surprised to find a nugget of compromise in their words.

If you are listening, you will find it easier to come to an agreement regarding the division of the property. I am not saying that listening with an open heart and mind will make the process any smoother, but it will help you to make better choices. The act of listening will allow for decisions to be made from a place of peace and not out of anger. After all, you both loved each other in the beginning, didn't you?

You built a life together on that first love. Even if you are now hurt, remember that the relationship did have value for you at one point. Only now, it is time to move on. Moving on may be difficult, but it is something positive. Look on the bright side. Showing respect to the other individual demonstrates not only the value you placed on that relationship and the respect you have for them, but more importantly, your respect for who you are as an individual, and the type of person you aim to be.

Granted, there may be points that you feel must be addressed, and there may be other things that you believe are not worth a compromise. This is the time to be clear about why you want specific items or financial arrangements. If you are insisting on some demands because you need them, and not because you don't want your partner to have them, be open and honest about it. Being honest helps you to make more logical decisions and find better solutions as you reach for resolutions with the other party.

An important part of this process also, is understanding what your peace of mind is worth. While you are fighting for your rights, you are also agitating yourself to the point that you are disrupting your own peace. Nothing is worth the sacrifice of your peace. Do not make the mistake of prioritizing the material and financial things of your relationship over your peace and safety. When you work from a place of peace, and are determined to leave the relationship, you will find that your act of being open-minded and of listening, play a pivotal role in preserving your peace.

Let's be honest here. They who were your partner may not now come into these relationship-closing discussions with good intentions toward you. They may be actively looking to do you harm, to drag out negotiations so that you bear the costs emotionally and financially. It is not easy to tell, but if you draw a mental line in the sand, it could help you find and blot out that place where you do not want to allow yourself to be taken. Be open to accepting when you have come to the point where you decide that the value of the assets is not higher than the value of your peace. Then be willing to let the material items go when that point is reached.

Start making these decisions in your mind before going into any negotiations, because if you become emotionally heated, you may decide to keep fighting long after you should have let go. On the other hand, if you had already made the decisions in your mind and heart regarding the best route to take, you can be at peace with saying, 'That's enough,' and be content with letting go and walking away.

As you prepare for the negotiations, bear in mind:

1. What your priorities are.

2. How respectful you need to be in your speech and actions.

3. To be true to your word. If you agree to something, then do what you say, even if it is now painful for you. Demonstrating integrity

will allow you to maintain your peace, rather than rob you of it.

4. To be willing to walk away from material things, not only to preserve your peace and safety, but also to avoid a drawn-out argument with your ex-partner, particularly if there are children in the equation. Children should not have to live with the reality of a long, bitter battle, just for one partner to have the victory over the other.

The process is not about winning or losing, but about finding your way through the challenges so you regain and maintain your peace of mind. To enter the discussions with the attitude of winning at all costs is to leave yourself scorched and parched in the end. It is unimaginable the damage that that attitude can do to you while you hold on to resentments and malice. It is even more devastating to your children, who you love so dearly, as you both fight in and out of court. When debates and disagreements are based on a win or lose attitude, they rarely stay contained to any negotiation room or any courthouse. They naturally spill over into every interaction that you have, especially those that are related to your children. And what is the worst thing that can happen? Your precious children, who you love so much, are tarnished with mental health issues for the rest of their lives.

Do the children deserve this negatively charged, very toxic environment? Should the children have to live in this environment perpetually? Do your precious little ones deserve to have to live like this for the short or long term? This lethal atmosphere is emotionally and mentally damaging to them. If you are caught up in such a battle with your now defunct partner, and you are finding that peace is not enough of a reason to stop the fight, then consider your children's need for peace, safety, and healthy minds, to help rein you in.

This now brings us into how to manage speech and actions around our children to protect them from experiencing mental or emotional barriers to one or either parent.

Creating Good Relationships for Your Children

The peace of your life also extends to the relationships that your children are going to have with you and your now ex-partner. Stopping to think for a moment about the position we put our children in, when we talk negatively about our partner with them or in their presence, will make us aware of how devastating this experience is for innocent minds and spirits. Without intending to, we, as adults, place children in positions where they feel that their parents' love for them is conditional upon their loyalty to one or either of their parents. Consequently, our children get trapped in the game of very efficiently playing one parent against the other, to their own loss and detriment.

An integral part of creating and maintaining peace in your broken relationships is choosing to let your children have a healthy relationship with both parents, without worrying about whether that puts their relationship with you in jeopardy. I believe this is the most important decision to be made when a relationship ends.

Always be willing to tell yourself that your peace of mind and heart is more important than anything, especially when you find yourself reacting to something that does not deserve your energy. If your partner does not work on their relationship with the children, then the children will, surprisingly, make their own decisions regarding that relationship, on their own without adult interference. You never want to put yourself in the position where you appear to be blocking your children from a relationship with their other parent.

Ultimately, if you are focused on the relationship of your children with your partner, to the point where you can't have peace with yourself, then pause to re-evaluate your situation. Ask yourself what is causing you to involve yourself in a negative way into the relationship of the children and their other parent?

Your personal peace also hinges on how you discuss and finalize the welfare of the children with your partner.

Though you are not together anymore, you are both still jointly and perpetually the parents of your children. That means you still need to work together to create consistency for your children as they transition from a one-family unit to a split arrangement. Consistency may not always be possible, but doing the best you can is required and desirable. Strive to build peace into your conversations always, because doing so will help you both to parent your children without bringing negativity into the picture.

Here are three rules to observe and maintain in your relationship with your children, during your divorce and for the years afterwards:

1. Always remember that words have a life and a power of their own. Measure them carefully, especially when speaking with your children.

2. Consciously and consistently encourage peace with your partner. Keep negative speech out of your interactions, regardless of the choices your partner makes.

3. Keep your love constant. Your children will grow into this constancy and will eventually see and feel that you truly love them. Your constancy will help them realize that they are not being disloyal to you while they grow their relationship with their other parent.

Each person has the power and the control to choose what to say and what to do. Our partner's or ex partner's behavior, words, and choices are also in their control. Therefore, never feed into a negative loop or try to beat out your ex-partner for a better relationship with your children. Just allow the relationships to flow. Be soft and gentle with your words. It is worth the effort and adds years to your life.

Leaving Safely and Staying Safe

If your relationship was marked by abuse of any type, shape, or color, do what is necessary to keep yourself and your children safe. Be willing to let go of the house and other material possessions to keep yourself and your children safe. Make safety your number one priority. There are many resources out there to help you safely exit an abusive relationship.

Part of the process of safely exiting a relationship includes creating an exit plan. Put those things in place that will allow you to be safe as you approach the end the relationship. A safety plan is a personalized, practical guideline, which includes ways to remain safe while you are still in the relationship, while you are planning to leave, and after you have left the relationship. The plan must be customized to your needs, and tailored to your unique situation, and may even include to-do lists for several different scenarios. Here are just a few things that you want to include in your safety plan:

- Tell family and friends about the abuse.

- Take legal action—speak with a lawyer who handles family, separation, and divorce issues.

- Find counseling and support to help you deal with your emotional responses.

- Practice the plan, and do it with your children.

- Show your children that violence is never right. Help them understand the importance of safety, and that you are doing everything to ensure their safety.

- Identify safe places to go, including family, or friends, or a shelter.

- Make use of emotional and mental support that is available in your community through your local church, community associations, or government services.

Keep in mind that when you are dealing with a volatile situation and your adrenaline is pumping, your brain is not going to function in the same way that it does when you are calm. Having a safety plan in place can help you navigate those stressful situations. All these efforts are to help you focus on finding calm and peace while you struggle to create a life that is free of violence and abuse.

The journey of leaving a violent and abusive relationship involves finding ways to build a support system. You may have been isolated by your partner, so reaching out to family and friends can be the first key steps to making your decision to leave. Then you should plan your exit in a timely, safe, and appropriate manner.

Dealing with Your Emotional and Mental Reactions

Throughout this journey, you may find that the importance of your emotional and mental states may be given second place, as you deal with the more practical aspects of ending your relationship. As those details are addressed and brought under control, you then need to take the time to rebuild your life and address those emotional and mental states that became disordered throughout the ordeal.

First, resolve to let go of the resentment that you may be harboring against your ex-partner. This is the process of making peace with the end of the relationship. Moments of grief may emerge over the loss of your status and stability that you worked hard to build together. That grief should not be ignored or downplayed. Speak with a counsellor or your religious leader. Do not keep these feelings to yourself. Get help right away, because you need a good sense of mental and emotional balance to continue to support yourself and your children properly.

Do not, therefore, allow the grief of the loss of your relationship to pull you down to the point that you are no longer living, but hiding away from the world. If you find yourself living in a state of depression, reach out for help, and deal with it. As part of that healing process, reconnect with your passions, your hobbies, and your cherished activities that bring you joy. You may also want to seriously consider counseling, especially if you are having trouble processing your emotional responses and reactions that relate to the ending of your relationship.

Coming to the decision to end your relationship is a long, emotional process. It is a mental and emotional roller coaster, with you hoping the relationship could be repaired, mourning for your dream that is now shattered, while trying to figure out how to end the relationship in a way that takes care of your needs. You are bombarded with thoughts that this was not what you bargained for, and now you have become a disastrous failure. In fact, you are none of those negatives. You are strong. You are courageous. You are invincible. You are alive and full of hope and promise. Your best is yet to come, and that is why you are now reading through the pages of this book.

Change is challenging, but change prompted by loss can be even more challenging. So, as you end the relationship, focus on the practical details of where to live, the needs of your children, and on the financial matters at hand. With your focus fully placed on these practical details, put the energy that is left, on building better emotional and mental states of being for yourself.

The choice to end a relationship is never easy. However, if you are sure you have reached this point, then it is time to spend your time and energy looking forward. You must now build a future for yourself with the resources that you now have available to you. Do not allow your emotional and mental responses from the grief of your relationship to put your future at risk.

Remember, nothing that you gain or lose materially from ending the relationship can be compared to the value of your peace of mind.

Finding Support

The journey to end a relationship with your partner involves several decisions along the way to help you build up your support system. This support can come from a variety of areas. Have a few close friends or family members to sit with you during the times of grief to help you get back into those worthy areas of your life that you may have neglected. Get them to listen to you, and be open to their hugs and their efforts to get you out of the house. Then, join them to enjoy life once again in a different way.

Also, consider looking for a support group made up of people who are dealing with ending their relationships. It is not safe to isolate yourself, as doing so can raise your stress levels and get in the way of your work, your other relationships, and your physical and mental health. Be flexible and open to finding new activities and friends while you create a new "normal" for your life. Avoid any form of power struggles or arguments with your former partner, and be open to walking away and to suggesting that discussions be postponed for a more convenient time.

Support will keep you from falling into bad habits that will have a negative impact on your life. If, for example, you are slipping into the habit of drinking alcohol to excess on a regular basis, this will bring you more negative consequences, and will not fix those feelings you are trying to rid yourself of. Focus rather on tapping into your coping skills in a positive way. Positive coping skills will lead you away from devastating consequences, and will help you make better of your life's circumstances.

The different forms of emotional and mental support that you find and use will help you navigate your transition back to being a single individual. As you gain your footing, be open to reaching out and helping others. Share your learning. Write it in a book or song or poem, for example. Leave your positive footprints on the sands of time. Eventually, you will be able to look back at the ending of your relationship with peace and calm. So, look forward now to the rest of your life, and start moving toward achieving your own personal goals and dreams.

NOTES

_____

_____

_____

_____

_____

_____

_____

_____

_____

_____

_____

_____

_____

11

The Journey of Relationships

11

Every part of my journey, so far, has been full of relationships. Some have been toxic. Others have been enriching. I find myself learning from both types, and they are helping me grow and glow. Throughout the pages of this book, I have shared my wisdom from this journey, and I hope that you are finding my testimonies and words of encouragement beneficial for your journey as well.

One of the biggest lessons for me was to find a space for peace in the most difficult times. When I was dealing with my rocky marriage and the toxicity of the relationship, I could have spent my time being angry, breaking things, putting blame on others, and inflicting myself. Instead, I infused my life with peace. I allowed peace to reign in my spirit. I sought after peace and wooed her with my words and my prayers. Conversations with others, and especially with my children, were massaged with the healing balm of peace and calm. It always amazed me when observers would exclaim repeatedly: "How can you be so calm? I could never do that; I would be pulling out my hair." Listen, my hair is my beauty, and I need it now and in the future. Why then would I destroy it for only one moment in time?

Can you think of areas in your life that are suffering because you are allowing the negativity of a present situation to eat away at your peace? In discussing relationship challenges, I focused on basic skills that you can use to create and build peace in your life and in your relationships. First, look for ways to improve communication. Be open to listening with your heart, in place of your mind. Make the conscious choice to listen for what your partner is intending to convey to you. Ask politely for clarification when you have questions. You will be surprised by how much you learn about your partner's intentions, feelings, hopes, and dreams when the communication is calm and polite. When you are more informed about your partner, it positively impacts your responses. Whatever you do, promise me to stay away from assumptions and accusations! They are the demons responsible for the breakup of good relationships.

While I focused on communication frequently throughout this book, I also want to start you on a path where you are consciously thinking about how you are treating those in your life. It surprises me how much is in our powers to shape our relationships with others by shifting how we respond to them. Could toxic relationships have been different if partners were to have engaged in positive conversational modes of solving their problems? As the saying goes, the proof is in the eating. Let's put it to the test. Relationship challenges take much effort on our part to retain the peace, but peace is worth the effort.

Identifying Challenges and Coming up with a Plan

Every journey has challenges that must be properly managed once they emerge. First, identify and note the challenges you could face, and then plan out ahead of time how you could address them before they appear.

I believe in thinking about challenges when my emotions are under control, because that is when I make better decisions and choices regarding the course of action that allows me to maintain the peace. The power to defy the odds against your peace, regardless of your situation, is in your hands. I suggest we fight for peace at all times. Our fight must include avoiding any discussions when we find ourselves in a heated emotional state. It is better to always aim for a calm and quiet time and place to talk without attacking others. Calm allows us to say the right things at the appropriate time. Therefore, if you find you are losing your calm, ask for a time out, or take it if you must. Walk away and work on resuming your composure. My grandfather always tells us, "He who fights and runs away, will live to fight another day." So, taking time away to process your emotions before continuing a heated discussion, is vital to maintaining your ability to listen attentively with your heart and mind. Throughout your own journey, then, remind yourself that you are indeed the guardian of your own peace. No matter what you are being confronted with, you have the right and the responsibility to protect your own mental and emotional peace.

Whenever possible, do not have discussions with your partner in a heated emotional state. Do your best to find a calm and quiet time and place where you can discuss things without attacking each other. Part of the reason for this is that both of you are less likely to say things that you regret. However, if you find yourself getting heated, do not be afraid to ask for a time out and walk away to get yourself into a calm state again.

Your effort to find peace in all your situations allows you to find the joy of life, regardless of your circumstances. Your life's challenges will be transformed into opportunities to learn and grow, instead of becoming stuck in a relationship that has become a dead end for you.

Find Out What Blocks You

Communication is only one aspect of relationships. It is only one powerful part of the relationships that you have with others. There is one relationship, though, that is more important than any other, and that is the one that you have with yourself. You, and only you, can give yourself permission to act or react in particular ways. Everything that you choose to do, every thought that you create, are all in existence because you gave yourself permission to produce them.

There is, however, the larger question of the relationship that you have with yourself. Are you telling yourself anything that is becoming a block in your life? Do you experience external blocks, or are they only internal ones? The words you use to yourself are an indication of what you will accept from others. If you are tolerant of negative talk from yourself, then you become open to negative talk from others with whom you relate. Negative self-talk, whether from yourself or from others, builds a strong block to positive personal growth and development. Negative talk is also indicative of the production or reception of the negative health of your relationships. Take a moment to evaluate and analyse your communication habits and traits. Are there areas requiring change and modification? Making changes will help you to dramatically improve your life and mental health.

Something else that can block your progress is the choice to stay in a relationship that is not healthy for you. Do you find that you are telling yourself that you do not deserve better? To do so is to block yourself from a healthier, happier, more peaceful life. On the other hand, being honest with yourself will help you find all potential blocks in your life, and start you on a different journey toward a more fulfilled, more worthwhile style of living.

In every chapter of this book, there are practical steps that you can use to address issues in your relationship and help you overcome your challenges. All the strategies provided will enable you to face your challenges and to understand yourself even better.

It is not necessarily about how you react to your aggravating partner that is at stake, but rather how you choose to respond internally before anything comes out of your mouth. Internal reactions open the doors to peace or otherwise block the very flow you so desire in your relationship.

Defensiveness, for example, is a reaction that keeps you from being honest with yourself. Often, defensiveness serves as a means of keeping people from making deeper connections with you, and from building trust in your relationships. Vulnerability, on the other hand, allows you to let down your walls of defense, and opens your mind and heart to deeper levels of trust that bolster and strengthen the growth of your relationships.

Other elements that stunt our ability to have a healthy relationship are secrecy and insincerity. Healthy relationships are built upon healthy interactions with individuals who are part of our life and our world. When we choose words and actions that attract others to us, we contribute to the harmony that debars the elements of division that hinder the growth of our relationships.

Throughout these chapters, I regularly refer to the power and ability you possess to create positive change in your life and your relationships. You have the capacity to change the dynamics of your relationships, even if the other person refuses to change. Finding out what blocks you is the key to better relationships. By uncovering and discovering your blocks, you put yourself in a position to take responsibility for your words, your actions, your choices, and your decisions. You do not put this responsibility on others. The joy and happiness we seek hinge on the decisions that we choose to make, and uncovering what our personal, individual blocks are is just the first step in the direction of our relationship progress and success. Once you determine what is blocking you, then the process of addressing those blocks begins.

Clearing Your Blocks

Your journey forward now depends on taking the knowledge of what your blocks are and consciously working to clear them. You might find it helpful to reach out to a life coach or a therapist to help you walk through the process. Try to incorporate clean habits as part of the block-clearing process. Take time each day for gratitude, journaling, and meditation. These are potent ways of building peace. This approach gives you the opportunity to process your challenges and find the calm necessary to communicate amicably with others.

Also, are you giving yourself a slot of time each day to unwind and de-stress mentally, emotionally, and physically? Nothing in your life is a waste, so learn and grow from your past relationships and experiences. Use them as catalysts to move you forward into your own next upward level.

Take time every day to write and put your thoughts in order, to help yourself address your challenges and limit toxicity. Positive foresight and outlook will help you unblock your previous and invaluable blockages, purify your thoughts, and clarify your vision.

I have talked often about the importance of writing as a form of communication, because writing gives you that opportunity to put your thoughts in order, and saves you from regretting something you would rather not have said or done. Writing or journaling is a way to pause before speaking, a strategy that quells harsh language and puts you on the cutting edge of self-control. Use it often. Use it well. Use it to your utmost advantage.

No matter what challenges you face in your relationships, you can create change that improves your relationship or ends it favorably. Favorably is what you want. Remember that your peace is most important, and that some relationships are not worth risking your peace. May your journey to achieve peace and contentment, as well as to manage the challenges of your relationships, be filled with experiences that continue to help you learn and grow.

I would love to hear how you have been able to stabilize your relationships by using the tips, principles, and tools found throughout this book. My goal in sharing my story and the knowledge gained from my experiences, is to inspire you and others to see the possibilities in your relationships, mainly by changing how you deal with others.

Please reach out to me through my website (www. couragebooknow.com). Let me know how you've been helped or how I can help you more. This journey is one that will continue throughout your life. I hope that every change will lead you on a path to peace, happiness, progress, prosperity, and success, in every area of your life! Shalom...

NOTES

_____

_____

_____

_____

_____

_____

_____

_____

_____

_____

_____

_____

_____

_____

About the Author

Jacinth Salmon-Brissett is an educator, author, and entrepreneur. She was born in the 1950s, with a hunger to read and write. She has spent years facilitating and accommodating students' diverse learning styles. Along the way, Jacinth has gathered a deep understanding of how personal relationships can grow and change, both positively and negatively.

In building her own interpersonal skills, Jacinth has gathered strategies and experiences that she has passed on to others. She continues to work in the field of education, with her latest position being teacher with the Calgary Board of Education.

Jacinth was born in Jamaica and has used many of the lessons learned there throughout her teaching and writing career. Today, she continues to teach, and also to grow her vacation rental business. Jacinth currently lives in Canada, where she immigrated with her children almost two decades ago.

To connect with Jacinth Salmon-Brissett,
please visit her website at:
www.couragebooknow.com.